STEAM CUISINE

D0480126

STEAM CUISINE

Jenny Stacey

FIREFLY BOOKS

641.73 S775 st

Stacey, Jenny
Steam cuisine

31120024302845

A FIREFLY BOOK

Published by Firefly Books Ltd. 1999

Copyright ©1999 Quintet Publishing Limited

All rights reserved. No part of this publication may be
reproduced, stored in a retrieval system, or transmitted in any
form or by any means, electronic, mechanical, photocopying,
recording, or otherwise, without the permission of the
copyright owner.

First Printing

Library of Congress Cataloguing
in Publication Data is available.

Canadian Cataloguing in Publication Data
Stacey, Jenny
Steam cuisine: full steam ahead with 100 delicious recipes
for a healthier diet

Includes index.
ISBN 1-55209-403-0

1. Steaming (Cookery). 2. Electric food steamers. 1. Title.
TX691.S74 1999 641.5'87 C99-930608-1

Published in Canada in 1999 by
Firefly Books Ltd.
3680 Victoria Park Avenue
Willowdale, Ontario
M2H 3K1

Published in the United States in 1999 by
Firefly Books (U.S.) Inc.
P.O. Box 1338, Ellicott Station
Buffalo, New York
14205

This book was designed and produced by
Quintet Publishing Limited
6 Blundell Street London N7 9BH

Creative Director: Richard Dewing
Art Director: Paula Marchant
Designer: Isobel Gillan and Rod Teasdale
Senior Editor: Sally Green
Editor: Margaret Gilbey

Food stylists: Eliza Baird and Emma Patmore
Photography: Ian Garlick and Howard Shooter
Typeset in Great Britain by
Central Southern Typesetters, Eastbourne

Manufactured in Hong Kong by
Regent Publishing Services Limited

Printed in China by
Leefung-Asco Printers Ltd.

The publishers would like to thank Divertimenti for the loan of a Pentole steamer.

CONTENTS

INTRODUCTION

Steaming, a cooking method thought to date back to before the discovery of fire, when foods were cooked over hot springs or stones, is now as popular as ever. Oriental cooking has always made great use of steaming as a main cooking method, both for health reasons and because ovens are very rare. Many foods are steamed, rather than baked, their main staple, rice, being perfect for this. The Chinese have used steamers for at least 3000 years or more, with early steamers being made in stoneware and originating in the province of Yunnan. From around the eighth century, thin cypress strips were used to make steamers and today they are constructed from bamboo with slatted bases. They may be stacked, usually up to three tiers, and placed over a wok containing boiling liquid. A tight-fitting bamboo lid seals in the steam.

The classic steamer contains a chimney through the center, which distributes the steam among the tiers. A variation on the theme is found in Hawaii, where for many years the Kalua or traditional pig roast has been steamed in a pit in the ground. Stones and wood are used to create and retain the heat in the pit, which is covered with layers of leaves. The pig is then cooked in the steam and smoke.

So as you can see, steaming is no quirky fad, rather a tried and tested, versatile and rewarding method of cooking. Gone are its associations with stodgy, bland foods — the true versatility and richness of steaming has been rediscovered. Healthier, more nutritious dishes may be easily prepared by steaming; the results are colorful and flavorful, textures fresh.

Suitable for most foods and a surprising variety of recipes, steaming has great advantages over other cooking methods. A far higher level of nutrients, vitamins and minerals is retained than by other cooking methods. Steam cooking reduces Vitamin C in vegetables by 40% whereas boiling reduces it by 70% because it is lost in the cooking water. Steaming does not immerse foods in water into which nutrients, particularly in vegetables, can escape. Foods are generally more nutritious when steamed, and as additional fat is not required for cooking it's also healthier and lower in fat. Even in recipes where higher fat content ingredients are called for, lower fat alternatives can generally be substituted, such as low-fat milk, cream and cheese, and poultry is always skinned to reduce fat content. Boiling does remain preferable for some vegetables such as mustard greens, turnip, collard greens or kale, which have strong flavors, as these may be imparted to other foods during steaming.

Steaming is a moist cooking method, using the natural convection of heat that is traveling in air, steam or liquid. This gives tender results because foods are not exposed to intense, dry heat as with other cooking methods. Steaming protects foods, which are contained within sealed, perforated or slatted tiers, wax paper or foil parcels or heatproof basins, and never come into contact with the heat source or steam-producing liquid. The tiers must sit at least 1 inch (2.5 cm) above the liquid so that it does not touch the food and overcook it. Steam produced from the heat of the liquid builds up inside the steamer, cooking food in a very moist atmosphere.

Flavorings may be added to foods in a variety of ways. Either in the cooking liquid, which may be water flavored with a bouillon cube or herbs and spices, fresh stock or wine, or by marinating foods before steaming. Spices such as ginger, chile, cumin and coriander may be added to savory recipes, and nutmeg, cinnamon, cloves and mint to sweet dishes. Herbs both fresh and dried, citrus juices, wines, spirits, oils, condiments and fruit juices may also be used to make interesting and flavor-enhancing marinades for many foods before steaming. It is therefore useful to always have a selection of these on hand. As the flavors are kept within the cooking vessel, the resulting dishes are quite intense and enjoyable. Simple steaming suggestions include flavoring vegetables with a squeeze of citrus juice or a sprinkling of chopped herbs, garlic or shallots, or a drizzle of flavored, good quality oil.

The three main methods of steaming

. The most popular and the quickest method for cooking meat, fish, vegetables, fruits and light desserts, is to suspend over boiling water, cover tightly and cook in the steam. This method may also be used for reheating and thawing foods.

. A longer method is cooking in a basin, bowl or paper or foil parcel over hot water. Foods are sealed within pleated wax paper or foil and secured with string. This is done to allow for expansion as the steam fills the parcel or basin. The string secures the paper to the basin and gives a tight fit to prevent steam escaping. Food cooks in its own juices, since the boiling water and steam do not come into direct contact with it. This method gives an exact and even cooking temperature throughout the cooking time, which is why it is used for melting chocolate and other tasks requiring consistent heat.

. In the Oriental method of steaming rice, which is used for dishes such as risotto and paella, the rice is immersed in water or stock, covered, and steamed until the liquid has been absorbed and the rice is cooked.

1

Water is added to the base of the saucepan.

2

For the longer method, foods are seated within pleated wax paper.

3

Cover the steamer tightly with its lid.

4

The Oriental method of cooking rice is perfect for dishes such as risotto and paella.

TYPES OF STEAMERS

All steamers follow the same basic principle whereby foods are cooked in perforated or slatted tiers above a deep pan of hot liquid, covered with a tight-fitting lid. Steam produced by the hot liquid cooks the food in the tiers above without having direct contact with it. The liquid may be water, wine, stock or an accompanying sauce, any flavors that you wish to have permeate the foods above. Use stock or salted water in the base of the steamer to simultaneously cook your pasta, rice or noodles to accompany a dish, but adjust cooking times to your preference for extra "bite."

There are three basic parts to a steamer: The first is a base compartment containing liquid which is heated to produce steam. The second is the steamer tier. The bottom is perforated so that steam can circulate around the food. There may be one or more of these, and if so the tiers stack on top of each other in order that different foods or courses may be steamed together without flavors combining. The third part of a steamer consists of a tight-fitting lid. This sits on top of either a single tier or the topmost tier and seals the whole unit,

Above left: *A good choice of electric steamers is now available.*

Above middle: *A stainless steel stovetop steamer. Several tiers may be acquired to make it even more versatile.*

Above right: *Chinese and bamboo steamers, which sit over a wok or saucepan, follow the same principle as other steamers.*

allowing steam to build up inside and cook the foods in a moist atmosphere. If the lid is not tight, cooking times will be a great deal longer and goodness will be lost during cooking. If using a pudding basin or dish to contain foods inside the tier, ensure that there is enough room to accommodate the juices that will build up during cooking.

Steaming is a radically different cooking method for some people and as such may require some adjusting to. To discover its true advantages takes time, but it is well worth pursuing. Begin by using a simple and inexpensive expanding, perforated metal basket or platform placed over a saucepan of hot liquid with a large roomy lid, large enough to allow steam to circulate around the food. A wok or Dutch oven will also work. This may be used to cook single layers of foods, although flavors cannot be separated, and is also good for reheating or thawing foods. However, the expanding basket takes up quite a lot of space in the pan and so is very limiting. A heatproof colander or two heatproof plates over a pan of boiling liquid are equally effective for this method of steaming.

A great advantage to the steaming method is that, since only one cooking pot is used for steaming, setting up and clear up times are greatly reduced, as is washing up! No precooking is required and foods may be left to cook without being watched over and stirred, so leaving you free to relax. You may prefer an electric steamer to a stovetop, which incorporates, among other things, a timer and thermostat for perfect and constant results. There is now a good choice of electric steamers available; virtually all of the major manufacturers of small kitchen appliances carry them in their product lines. They are quite large appliances which stand on the worktop, keeping the stove free. They have the advantage of several stacking tiers so that complete meals may be cooked, and can generally take larger cuts of meat and whole poultry. A thermostatically controlled element in the base of the steamer heats the water or stock and a timer switches the appliance off when cooking is complete. Specific rice steamers are often included, and drip trays that catch juices for making sauces and gravies.

In the 1950s, the High Rise Multi-Cooker, a low-tech steamer that could cook several different layers of food at one time, was introduced on one of television's first cooking shows. Since then models have greatly improved, and now steamers are made from stainless steel, the stovetop steamer being a common sight in the home. Several tiers may be acquired to make the standard steamer more versatile and as functional as an electric steamer, but only two to three levels is recommended.

Usually about 8 inches (20 cm) in diameter, the stovetop steamer will amply hold a meal for the average family. A handle either side allows for easy lifting, and many have a thermocore base made from sandwiched aluminum and stainless steel to take up heat quickly and prevent hot spots, which can lead to burning. The disadvantages to these cookers over the electric steamers is that you cannot see inside the tiers during cooking, which means either opening the lid and losing some of the steam's efficiency, or relying solely on recommended cooking times. It is preferable to take the latter route and not to lift the lid during cooking. Stovetop steamers also of course use a ring on the stove, which you may require for other, simultaneous cooking.

Chinese and bamboo steamers with slatted bases work on the same principle as all of the others. There are different sizes available, with two or three tiers topped with a solid lid. These sit over a wok, which usually contains either hot water or stock.

All of the recipes in the following chapters were tested in a stainless steel, stovetop, tiered steamer; cooking times are given as a guideline. Adjust times according to personal preference and to your model of steamer, following manufacturer's instructions. Bamboo, metal basket and colander steamers would produce approximately the same cooking times.

I have tried to bring you steaming at its best, using a wide variety of fresh, colorful and flavorsome ingredients in a great number of ways, both for your enjoyment and to demonstrate the versatility and full advantages of steaming. Most of us strive for healthy, tasty and easily prepared meals, and I guarantee that once you've dipped into this book and tried a few dishes, your diet will change for the better. Your cooking will be revolutionized.

Below: *The simple and inexpensive expanding metal basket is the best steamer with which to start.*

SOME GENERAL RULES

There are a few rules which should be followed when steaming to obtain perfect results every time:

• Ensure the ingredients used are of the best quality and in perfect condition. Choose lean meats which will be tender and not require lengthy cooking. Trim away excess fat before using and always cut across the grain for extra tenderness.

• Ensure the lid fits well to prevent the steam escaping and thus prolonging cooking time.

• When choosing fruit and vegetables, look for unblemished skins and good color. Do not use "old" or bruised fruits, because steaming enhances flavors and aromas and any slight taint in a food will be accentuated.

• Make sure foods to be cooked together are of a similar or even size so that they will cook in the same amount of time. This applies to chopped foods and meat, fish or poultry portions.

• Do not allow the liquid in the base compartment to touch the food, or the food will boil and not steam. Suspend it at least 1 inch (2.5 cm) above the liquid.

• Liquid levels in the base of the steamer should be maintained for constant cooking, although it should never be more than two-thirds full. Top up with boiling liquid to maintain cooking.

• Cook food in a single layer or adjust cooking times accordingly, as cooking will be slower.

• Arrange foods in the steamer compartment with space in between to allow steam to circulate and cook more efficiently. Always defrost frozen meats, fish and poultry before cooking, to allow for correct and complete cooking within the recommended times.

• Place meats, fish, or juicy foods in the bottom tiers so that they cannot drip onto foods below.

• Allow an extra five minutes for foods cooked in upper tiers because they are further away from the steam.

• Finally, be sure to continue cooking foods that are not cooked through or not cooked to your liking, despite having been cooked for the recommended cooking time.

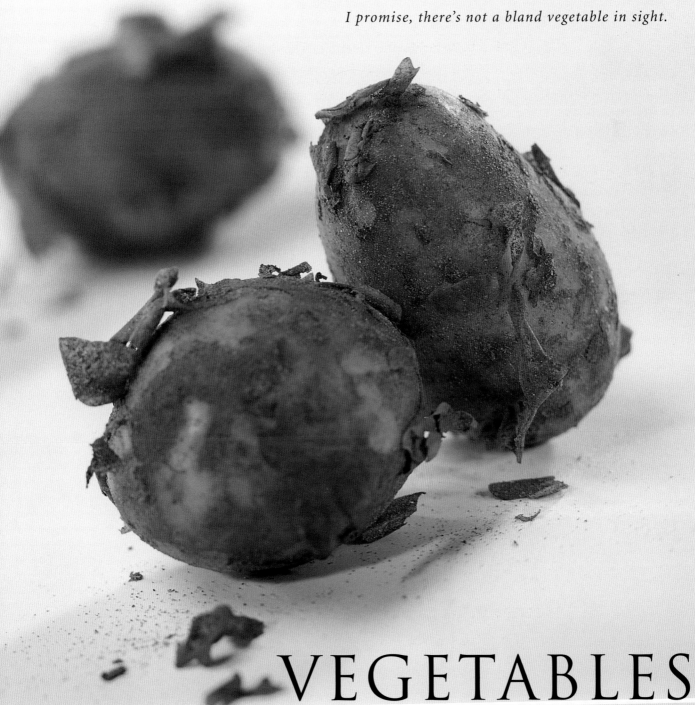

*M*ost people think of boring, bland vegetables when they think of steaming, but you are about to discover that this could not be further from the truth.

The only real way to cook vegetables successfully, for the best texture, color, flavor and nutritional value, is steaming. Many imaginative dishes filled with the flavors from herbs, marinades and sauces follow in this chapter. There are main courses, accompaniments and snacks for all tastes and occasions — I promise, there's not a bland vegetable in sight.

VEGETABLES

Marinating the vegetables brings out their flavors without overpowering. This dish may be prepared in advance and stored in the refrigerator for up to 4 hours.

MIXED VEGETABLE PASTA

Serves 4

1 medium leek, halved and shredded

1 medium red bell pepper, halved and thinly sliced

1 medium green bell pepper, halved and thinly sliced

1 medium orange bell pepper, halved and thinly sliced

8 baby corn, halved lengthwise

½ cup (100 mL) broccoli florets

4 Tbsp (50 mL) fava beans

2 Tbsp (25 mL) pitted black olives, whole

¾ cup (150 mL) dry white wine

3 garlic cloves, peeled and crushed

4 Tbsp (50 mL) olive oil

1 Tbsp (15 mL) walnut oil

3 Tbsp (45 mL) fresh mixed herbs, chopped

1 tsp (5 mL) dried chile peppers, chopped

1 cup (250 mL) spaghettini

❶ Place all of the prepared vegetables in a shallow glass dish. Mix the remaining ingredients together, except the spaghettini, and pour over the vegetables. Cover and leave to marinate for 2 hours, turning occasionally.

❷ Remove the vegetables and marinade from the dish and transfer to a wax paper-lined steamer tier.

❸ Bring salted water to a boil in the base of the steamer and add the pasta. Place the vegetables over the top, cover with a tight-fitting lid and steam for 10 minutes or until the pasta and vegetables are cooked. Check the pasta before 10 minutes if you prefer a firmer texture.

❹ Drain the pasta and place in a warm serving bowl. Spoon the vegetables on top, season, and serve immediately.

If preferred, substitute dried beans, which have been soaked overnight and boiled rapidly for 10 minutes before use. This has to be done to remove toxins in the beans, which should be rinsed well before adding to the recipe.

MIXED BEANS WITH RICE

Serves 4

15 oz (426 mL) can red kidney beans, drained

15 oz (426 mL) can black-eyed peas, drained

¾ cup (150 mL) vegetable stock

2 Tbsp (25 mL) Worcestershire or light soy sauce

2 Tbsp (25 mL) tomato paste

15 oz (426 mL) can chopped tomatoes

Few drops Tabasco Sauce

1 medium red onion, cut into eight

2 celery ribs, thickly sliced

3 garlic cloves, peeled and crushed

1 medium green bell pepper, thinly sliced

1 cup (250 mL) sweet potato, cubed

½ cup (100 mL) canned artichoke hearts, halved

For the rice

½ cup (100 mL) long-grain and wild rice, mixed

1 cup (200 mL) vegetable stock

1 cup (250 mL) spinach leaves, washed

1 Put all the ingredients except the rice and stock in a deep bowl. Cover with pleated foil secured with string, and place in the steamer top.

2 Bring the vegetable stock to a boil in the base of the steamer. Place the vegetables on top, cover, and steam for 25 minutes.

3 Add the rice to the stock and cook for 15 minutes. Stir in the spinach and continue cooking for a further 3 to 5 minutes until the vegetables and rice are tender. Serve.

This is a pie with a difference; the crust consisting of a cheese-flavored polenta batter is a wonderful topping for the colorful vegetable selection.

POLENTA PIE

Serves 4

½ small leek, shredded lengthwise
1 small carrot, cut into julienne strips
½ medium fennel bulb, thinly sliced
1 small red bell pepper, thinly sliced
½ small zucchini, cut into julienne strips
1 small tomato, seeded and cut into strips
2 Tbsp (25 mL) pitted black olives, quartered
2 Tbsp (25 mL) olive oil
Juice and zest of 1 medium lemon
1 garlic clove, peeled and crushed
1 Tbsp (15 mL) fresh oregano, chopped
Freshly ground black pepper

For the batter
6 Tbsp (75 mL) all-purpose flour
6 Tbsp (75 mL) polenta or cornmeal
1½ tsp (7 mL) baking powder
Pinch of salt
1 egg, beaten
¾ cup (150 mL) milk
2 Tbsp (25 mL) freshly grated
Parmesan cheese
4 scallions, finely chopped

❶ Put all of the prepared vegetables in a shallow glass dish. Mix the oil, lemon juice and zest, garlic, herbs and black pepper together, and pour over the vegetables, turning to coat. Cover and leave to marinate for 1 hour, turning occasionally.

❷ Sift the flour into a mixing bowl and add the polenta, baking powder, and salt. Mix the egg and milk together. Make a well in the center of the dry mixture and gradually whisk in the egg and milk to make a smooth batter. Stir in the cheese and onions, and season well.

❸ Remove the vegetables from the marinade and spoon into the base of a lightly greased 2 pint (1L) casserole dish. Pour the batter on top and cover in pleated foil secured with string.

❹ Place the basin in the top of the steamer, cover, and steam for 50 minutes until the batter is set. Serve immediately with potatoes or rice and a green salad.

This is a filling dish which may be made with a variety of nuts for an equally good result. Try pecans or walnuts as an alternative. If possible, allow the loaf to stand for 10 minutes before slicing.

CASHEW AND ASPARAGUS BOMBE

Serves 4

1 Tbsp (15 mL) olive oil

1 medium red onion, chopped

2 garlic cloves, peeled and crushed

¾ cup (170 mL) unsalted cashews, finely chopped

6 Tbsp (75 mL) whole wheat bread crumbs

1 egg, beaten

1 large potato, peeled, cooked and mashed

2 Tbsp (25 mL) fresh mixed herbs, chopped

1 tsp (5 mL) yeast extract

¾ cup (150 mL) vegetable stock

¾ cup (150 mL) asparagus spears

For the sauce

¾ cup (150 mL) vegetable stock

1 Tbsp (15 mL) tomato paste

3 Tbsp (45 mL) dry sherry

2 Tbsp (25 mL) butter

❶ Heat the oil in a pan and sauté the onion and garlic for 2 to 3 minutes until beginning to soften. Add the nuts and bread crumbs.

❷ Remove from the heat and stir in the egg, potato, herbs, yeast extract and stock. Mix well and press half the mixture into the base of a 3½-cup (900 mL) pudding dish or mold lined with wax paper, which fits into the steamer tier.

❸ Arrange the asparagus spears on top and spoon on remaining cashew mixture. Cover with pleated wax paper and secure with string.

❹ Steam the loaf in the top of a steamer for 1 hour or until set. Leave to stand for 10 minutes before turning out and slicing.

❺ Meanwhile, heat the stock, tomato paste and sherry for the sauce, and bring to a boil. Gradually whisk in the butter and serve with the sliced loaf.

These mushrooms hint of Mexican cuisine and are surprisingly simple to prepare. They make an ideal lunch with salad, sour cream and fresh bread.

STUFFED MUSHROOMS

Serves 4

8 large opencap mushrooms,
   peeled and cleaned
4 Tbsp (50 mL) whole wheat bread crumbs
4 scallions, chopped
1 ripe avocado, finely chopped
1 small red chile pepper, sliced
1 large tomato, seeded and chopped
2 tsp (10 mL) lemon juice
4 Tbsp (50 mL) freshly grated
   mozzarella cheese
1 Tbsp (15 mL) fresh cilantro, chopped

❶ Remove the stalks from the mushrooms and chop finely. Stir into the bread crumbs, scallions, avocado, chile pepper, tomato and lemon juice, mixing well.

❷ Spoon the mixture onto the mushroom caps, piling up, pressing and shaping with a spoon, so the mounds hold together. Sprinkle the cheese on top, then the cilantro.

❸ Place the mushroom caps in the steamer top, cover with the lid, and steam for 10 minutes until tender. Serve with salad.

This dish is full of Mediterranean flavors and makes a great snack or side dish. Vegetable marrow could be used in place of zucchini. This dish is also ideal cold with meats or fish, as a salad. When young, the whole eggplant is tender and wonderfully edible; older eggplant should be peeled. Overripe eggplant can also be salted heavily and left to drain 20 minutes, to reduce the fruit's bitterness (eggplant is technically a berry)

GARLIC, ZUCCHINI AND EGGPLANT

Serves 4

2 cups (500 mL) zucchini
2 large eggplants, halved and thickly sliced
2 medium leeks, thickly sliced
4 garlic cloves, peeled and crushed
15 oz (426 mL) can artichoke hearts,
   drained and halved
4 Tbsp (50 mL) olive oil
Freshly ground black pepper
1 Tbsp (15 mL) fresh mixed herbs, chopped

❶ Salt the eggplant if desired. Mix together the eggplant, zucchini, leeks, garlic, artichoke hearts, oil, black pepper and herbs. Stir well and transfer to a foil-lined steamer tier.

❷ Cover with a tight-fitting lid and steam for 45 minutes or until the vegetables are tender. Serve with steamed rice or as an accompaniment to plain meats.

Red split lentils are a great staple ingredient to keep on hand, as they require no presoaking and add great flavor, fiber and many essential nutrients including calcium, vitamins A and D, iron and phosphorous.

LENTIL PILAF

Serves 4

1 Tbsp (15 mL) oil
4 scallions, finely chopped
¾ cup (175 mL) dry red lentils
1 cup (250 mL) basmati rice
1 tsp (5 mL) turmeric
1 medium carrot, grated
1 medium red bell pepper, finely diced
2 Tbsp (25 mL) sultana raisins
½ cup (100 mL) French beans,
 finely chopped
1 celery rib, finely diced
1 tsp (5 mL) chile powder
1 tsp (5 mL) fennel seeds
1 tsp (5 mL) ground cumin
1 Tbsp (15 mL) fresh cilantro, chopped
2½ cups (600 mL) vegetable stock

For the sauce
2½ cups (600 mL) puréed tomatoes
1 medium onion, finely chopped
2 garlic cloves, peeled and crushed
1 Tbsp (15 mL) fresh cilantro, chopped
Salt and freshly ground black pepper

❶ Place all of the pilaf ingredients in the base of the steamer, cover, and cook for 30 minutes until the stock has been absorbed.

❷ Spoon the mixture into ramekins or molds, and place in a steamer tier.

❸ Wash out the base of the steamer and put in all of the sauce ingredients. Stack the tier with the pilaf molds on top and cover with a tight-fitting lid.

❹ Bring the sauce to a boil, reduce the heat slightly, and cook for 10 minutes.

❺ Turn the rice molds out onto warm serving plates and spoon the sauce around the base. Garnish with cilantro and serve.

A favorite Mexican dish, these irresistible tortillas are a great informal supper dish. Use any good combination of vegetables that you have on hand.

SPICY VEGETABLES IN TORTILLAS

Serves 4

1 medium onion, quartered and thinly sliced

4 baby corn, halved lengthwise

2 celery ribs, cut into julienne strips

1 medium zucchini, cut into julienne strips or thinly sliced

4 Tbsp (50 mL) snow peas, sliced

1 medium red bell pepper, cut into strips

2 large tomatoes, seeded and cubed

1 medium green chile pepper, thinly sliced

1 garlic clove, peeled and crushed

2 Tbsp (25 mL) tomato paste

¾ cup (150 mL) vegetable stock

2 Tbsp (25 mL) fresh cilantro, chopped

1 tsp (5 mL) ground coriander

8 flour tortillas, frozen or fresh

¾ cup (150 mL) plain yogurt

❶ Mix all of the vegetables together in a heatproof bowl and place in the top of the steamer.

❷ Mix the tomato paste, stock, 1 tablespoon (15 mL) chopped cilantro and ground coriander together, and pour over the vegetables in the bowl. Cover with pleated wax paper and steam for 15 minutes until the vegetables are tender.

❸ Lay the tortillas in the base of the second tier of the steamer and place over the vegetables for the last 5 minutes of cooking time or until warmed through.

❹ Mix the yogurt and remaining cilantro in a serving bowl.

❺ Spoon the vegetable mixture into the tortillas and serve with yogurt.

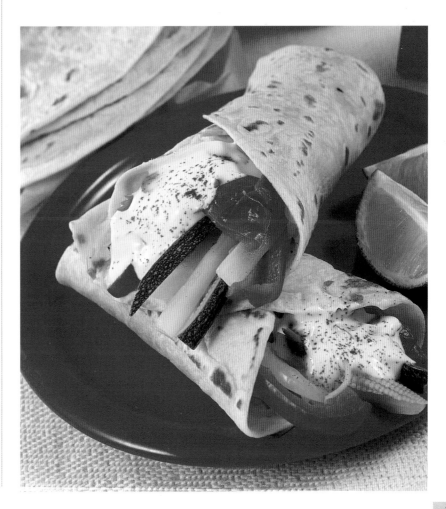

Hot salads are a delicious alternative and can be served as a meal with hot crusty bread or as a side dish. Be sure to serve it immediately as the chicory browns very quickly.

STEAMED CHICORY SALAD

Serves 4

4 large heads chicory
1 medium carrot, cut into julienne strips
3 scallions, shredded
1-in (2.5 cm) piece fresh ginger, shredded
2 Tbsp (25 mL) pine nuts
2 Tbsp (25 mL) freshly grated
   Parmesan cheese
Freshly ground black pepper

For the dressing
3 Tbsp (45 mL) walnut oil
2 Tbsp (25 mL) lemon juice
1 Tbsp (15 mL) liquid honey
2 Tbsp (25 mL) fresh mixed herbs, chopped
1 Tbsp (15 mL) balsamic vinegar

❶ Separate the chicory heads into individual leaves, rinse and dry, and arrange in the centers of four large squares of wax paper.

❷ Add the carrot, scallions, ginger and pine nuts.

❸ Mix the dressing ingredients, shaking well. Bring the sides of each waxed square up to make a parcel and pour ¼ of the dressing into each parcel. Seal and place in the top of the steamer.

❹ Steam for 10 minutes until hot. Open the parcels and sprinkle the cheese over the top. Season and serve immediately with hot bread.

This is a really simple side dish which is great with poultry or fish. Cucumber and peas or other varieties of bean will work equally well.

ZUCCHINI AND BEANS WITH GARLIC AND MINT

Serves 4

2 large zucchini, thickly sliced
½ cup (100 mL) green beans, thickly sliced
2 tsp (10 mL) lemon juice
1 Tbsp (15 mL) fresh mint, chopped
2 garlic cloves, peeled and crushed
2 Tbsp (25 mL) butter
Salt and freshly ground black pepper
Fresh mint sprigs and lemon zest, to garnish

❶ Cut a large square of foil and place the vegetables in the center. Fold up sides, without closing, to a size that will fit in your steamer.

❷ Top the vegetables with the lemon juice, mint, garlic, butter and seasoning, and close the foil around the vegetables to form a parcel, sealing well.

❸ Place the parcel in the steamer tier over boiling water. Cover with a tight-fitting lid and steam for 8 to 10 minutes until the vegetables are tender. Garnish and serve.

Goat cheese gives a strong and distinctive flavor to bell peppers, and is steamed until just melted to perfection. Serve with a green salad for a very colorful dish.

GOAT CHEESE-FILLED PEPPERS

Serves 4

2 medium red bell peppers
2 medium yellow bell peppers

For the filling
1½ cups (350 mL) goat cheese
2 Tbsp (25 mL) pine nuts
2 garlic cloves, peeled and crushed
2 Tbsp (25 mL) pimiento-stuffed
   green olives, chopped
2 celery ribs, thinly sliced
2 Tbsp (25 mL) fresh parsley, chopped
2 Tbsp (25 mL) raisins

❶ Bring water to a boil in the base of the steamer. Cut each of the bell peppers in half lengthwise and remove the core and seeds. Blanch the peppers for a scant 5 minutes in the water and then remove with a slotted spoon.

❷ Mix the remaining ingredients together and spoon into the bell pepper shells. Place in the base of the steamer top over the boiling water. Cover tightly and steam for 20 minutes. Serve with a crisp green salad.

You may use fresh artichokes in this recipe if preferred but, for speed and ease, canned artichoke hearts are just as delicious. This is an ideal side dish for grilled or steamed chicken.

MEDITERRANEAN ARTICHOKES

Serves 4

14 oz (398 mL) can artichoke hearts, drained
3 garlic cloves, peeled and crushed
1 large onion, cut into 16
1 Tbsp (15 mL) butter
2 Tbsp (25 mL) Madeira
1 cup (250 mL) chopped fresh or
   canned tomatoes
1 Tbsp (15 mL) tomato paste
1 tsp (5 mL) brown sugar
2 Tbsp (25 mL) fresh basil or
   marjoram, chopped
2 Tbsp (25 mL) black pitted olives, halved

❶ Cut the artichoke hearts into halves.

❷ Place all of the ingredients in a heatproof dish which fits a steamer tier. Cover snugly with pleated foil and with a tight-fitting lid.

❸ Steam for 20 minutes or until the vegetables are tender. Serve immediately.

Individual timbales are ideal as a dinner party appetizer. Be sure to press any excess moisture from the spinach before combining with the eggs otherwise the resulting dish will be very watery.

ASPARAGUS TIMBALE

Serves 4

1 cup (250 mL) asparagus tips

1 small leek, thinly sliced

1 cup (250 mL) spinach leaves, washed

1 large opencap mushroom, peeled, cleaned and chopped (about ¼ cup)

2 garlic cloves, peeled and crushed

1 Tbsp (15 mL) fresh thyme, chopped

6 eggs, beaten

2 Tbsp (25 mL) freshly grated Parmesan cheese

Salt and freshly ground black pepper

Asparagus spears and grated Parmesan cheese, to garnish

❶ Place the vegetables, garlic, and thyme in the base of a steamer tier over boiling water. Cover and steam for 10 minutes.

❷ Transfer the vegetables to a food processor or blender and purée for 30 seconds until smooth. Beat in the eggs and cheese. Season well.

❸ Spoon the mixture into four ramekins, cover each with pleated wax paper, secured with string. Place the dishes in the top of the steamer and cook over boiling water for 40 minutes until set. Garnish with asparagus spears blanched until tender and Parmesan cheese. Serve with hot toasted bread according to taste.

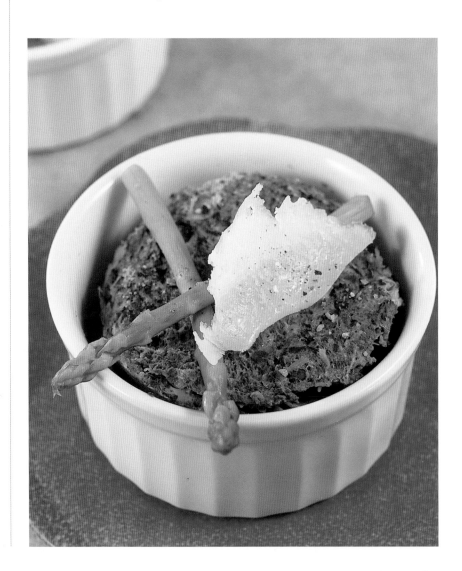

These stuffed eggplants can be served as a main meal or as an appetizer, if the recipe is halved in quantity. Tahini dip is available from gourmet food stores and makes an ideal accompaniment.

MIDDLE EASTERN EGGPLANT

Serves 4

4 small eggplants
4 Tbsp (50 mL) couscous
1 garlic clove, peeled and crushed
2 tsp (10 mL) light brown sugar
1 medium tomato, roughly chopped
4 Tbsp (50 mL) dried apricots, finely chopped
2 Tbsp (25 mL) blanched almonds, chopped
2 Tbsp (25 mL) fresh cilantro, chopped
2 scallions, finely chopped
1 tsp (5 mL) ground coriander
Salt and freshly ground black pepper
Tahini dip, to serve

1 Cut the eggplant in half lengthwise and sprinkle liberally with salt. Leave to stand in a sieve, flesh down, for 20 minutes, then rinse under cold water. Pat dry.

2 Meanwhile, soak the couscous in boiling water for 20 minutes. Drain off any excess liquid.

3 Scoop the flesh out of the eggplant, leaving a thin lining in the skin. Chop the flesh coarsely and mix with the couscous, garlic, sugar, tomato, apricots, almonds, cilantro, scallions and ground coriander. Season well.

4 Spoon the mixture into the eggplant shells and place in the steamer tiers. Cover with a tight-fitting lid and steam for 15 to 20 minutes. Serve hot with tahini dip and salad.

Fresh baby vegetables have a fresh flavor all their own. In this dish they are served simply, with a yogurt and garlic sauce and plain pasta. Use any combination of mixed vegetables that you have on hand for a spur of the moment dish.

FETTUCCINE PRIMAVERA

Serves 4

1¼ cups (300 mL) fettuccine

6 Tbsp (75 mL) broccoli florets

4 baby carrots, halved lengthwise

1 medium red bell pepper, cubed

1 medium green bell pepper, cubed

1 medium red onion, quartered and
   thinly sliced

4 Tbsp (50 mL) fava beans

2 Tbsp (25 mL) peas

2 garlic cloves, peeled and crushed

6 Tbsp (75 mL) freshly grated Cheddar cheese

5 Tbsp (65 mL) plain yogurt

Pinch of cayenne pepper

Salt and freshly ground black pepper

❶ Bring a large quantity of salted water to a boil in the base of the steamer and add the pasta.

❷ Place all of the vegetables in a wax paper-lined steamer tier, cover with a tight-fitting lid, and steam over the pasta for 10 minutes. Check the pasta before 10 minutes to ensure it does not overcook.

❸ Add the cheese, yogurt and cayenne pepper to the vegetables and keep warm.

❹ Drain the pasta and transfer to a warm serving dish. Top with the vegetables, season well, and serve immediately.

Poppy seeds give a great flavor to these glazed vegetables, but other seeds such as fennel may be used to vary the taste. A perfect accompaniment to marinated lamb or pork.

HONEY-GLAZED VEGETABLES

Serves 4

2 medium baby turnips, trimmed and halved

2 medium carrots, cut into julienne strips

2 celery ribs, cut into julienne strips

1 large zucchini, cut into julienne
strips or sliced thinly

4 baby corn, halved lengthwise

3 Tbsp (45 mL) liquid honey

2 Tbsp (25 mL) vegetable stock

2 tsp (10 mL) light soy sauce

2 tsp (10 mL) poppy seeds

Salt and freshly ground black pepper

❶ Place all of the vegetables in a shallow dish. Mix the honey, stock and soy sauce, and pour over the vegetables.

❷ Sprinkle the poppy seeds over the vegetables, turning them to coat well.

❸ Place the vegetables in a wax paper-lined steamer tier and cover with a tight-fitting lid.

❹ Steam for 20 minutes or until the vegetables are tender. Season with salt and freshly ground black pepper.

Beets are a very nutritious but often neglected vegetable. Choose small to medium beets as these will be more tender. Remove the leaves (also edible and very nutritious) as soon as you get home, as the leaves leach nutrients from the beet root. Leave on about 1 inch of stem; this helps retain the nutrients while cooking. Peel after cooking. This beet dish is packed with color and flavor, and should be served as a side dish with a milder entrée or as an appetizer with a crisp green salad. It may be made in advance and left to chill in the refrigerator until required (up to 4 hours). Peaches or nectarines can be used in place of the oranges.

SPICY BABY BEETS AND ORANGE

Serves 4

10 small beets, gently washed

¾ cup (150 mL) orange juice

¾ cup (150 mL) red wine

2 Tbsp (25 mL) garlic vinegar

2 tsp (10 mL) liquid honey

2 scallions, thickly sliced

Orange zest and segments, to garnish

❶ Place the beets in the steamer, cover with a tight-fitting lid, and steam over the orange juice, wine, vinegar, honey and scallions for 15 to 20 minutes until the beets are fork-tender.

❷ Remove the beets, and set aside. Bring the liquid to a boil until thickened. Meanwhile, peel the beets and slice into rounds.

❸ Arrange the beets on warm serving plates and spoon the sauce over the top. Garnish and serve immediately.

New potatoes are just young potatoes, of any variety. Choose firm, well-shaped and blemish-free potatoes of roughly equal size, so that they all cook in the same amount of time.

GARLIC NEW POTATOES

Serves 4

2 cups (450 mL) new potatoes,
  lightly scrubbed
2 Tbsp (25 mL) olive oil
2 garlic cloves, peeled and crushed
1 Tbsp (15 mL) fresh basil, chopped

For the sauce
1 small onion, quartered and thinly sliced
1 tsp (5 mL) paprika
Pinch of cayenne pepper
1 tsp (5 mL) fennel seeds
1¼ cups (300 mL) puréed tomatoes
1¼ cups (300 mL) vegetable stock
2 Tbsp (25 mL) fresh basil, chopped
1 tsp (5 mL) brown sugar
Fresh basil, to garnish

❶ Line a steamer tier with foil, making an edge to form a dish. Put the potatoes, oil, garlic and basil in the foil.

❷ Place the sauce ingredients in the base of the steamer and bring to a boil. Cook the potatoes, covered, over the sauce for 45 minutes until the potatoes are tender. Garnish with basil, and serve with the sauce.

Bell peppers have their own special flavor, especially when marinated and steamed in this lovely combination of ingredients. They may be served over steamed rice if preferred to noodles.

CHILE-MARINATED BELL PEPPERS OVER NOODLES

Serves 4

1 large green bell pepper
1 large red bell pepper
1 large yellow bell pepper
1 large orange bell pepper
1 medium red chile pepper
2 garlic cloves, peeled and crushed
2 Tbsp (25 mL) soy sauce
2 Tbsp (25 mL) liquid honey
1 Tbsp (15 mL) dry sherry
Juice of 1 medium lime
1 Tbsp (15 mL) fresh rosemary
Freshly ground black pepper
4 cups (1 L) vegetable stock
1 cup (250 mL) egg noodles

1 Remove the seeds from the bell peppers and cut into cubes. Place in a shallow glass dish which fits the steamer, with the remaining ingredients except the noodles, cover, and leave to marinate for 1 hour, turning occasionally.

2 Transfer the dish to the steamer, cover with a tight-fitting lid, and cook over boiling stock for 15 minutes.

3 Add the noodles to the stock in the base of the steamer. Cook a further 5 minutes until the peppers are tender. Drain the noodles and place in a warmed serving bowl. Spoon the bell peppers on top and serve immediately.

Fish and seafood are among the best sources of protein available to us, and most are low in fats. The fats found in fish are polyunsaturated and therefore healthier than animal fats.

There are so many varieties of fish and shellfish to choose from, the world really is "your oyster" when choosing delicious recipes to cook, and steaming is the ideal cooking method. A moist method which requires no additional fat, it seals in all of the goodness to give us seafood at its best.

In this chapter I have tried to use a wide choice of fish and shellfish, but most recipes are interchangeable to accommodate your favorites. There are simple suppers, light lunches and special dishes for those more important occasions. I'm sure you will agree that steamed fish is just superb.

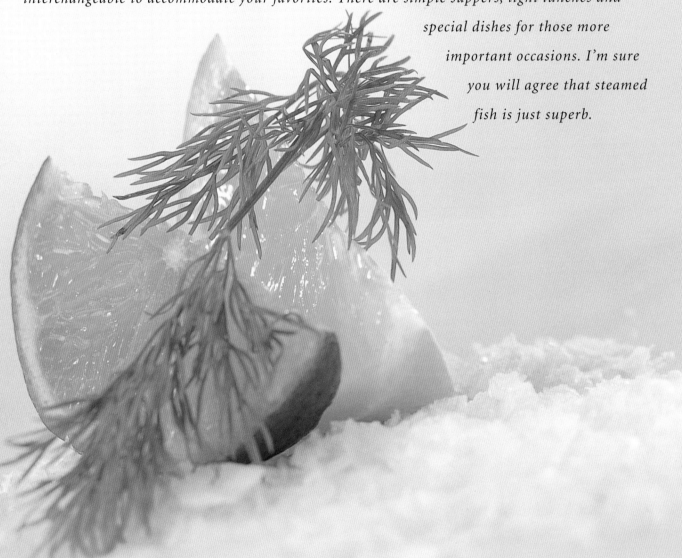

FISH & SHELLFISH

The bacon and orange in this stuffing are perfect partners to the wonderful full flavor of steamed trout. Citrus fruits are an ideal accompaniment for oily fish. Grapefruit could also be used.

COUSCOUS-STUFFED TROUT

Serves 4

4 whole trout (about 8 oz/225 g each), cleaned
1 large Romaine lettuce, washed and separated

For the stuffing
½ cup (100 mL) couscous
2 Tbsp (25 mL) butter
1 Tbsp (15 mL) olive oil
2 slices smoked bacon, finely chopped
1 small leek, finely chopped
¼ cup (50 mL) mushrooms, cleaned and
   finely chopped
1 small orange, peeled, segmented
   and chopped
2 Tbsp (25 mL) pine nuts
2 Tbsp (25 mL) fresh cilantro, chopped

❶ Wash the trout inside and out, under cold running water. Pat dry with paper towels and set aside.

❷ Soak the couscous in boiling water for 10 minutes until swollen. Drain and transfer to a lined steamer top, cover with a tight-fitting lid and steam over hot water for 15 minutes until softened. Stir in half the butter.

❸ Meanwhile, heat the olive oil with the remaining butter in a skillet and sauté the bacon and leek for 5 minutes. Add the mushrooms and cook for a further 2 minutes.

❹ Spoon the mixture into the couscous together with the orange, pine nuts and cilantro. Mix thoroughly.

❺ Using a spoon, stuff the cavity of each trout with a quarter of the stuffing, pressing it in with the back of the spoon.

❻ Steam the lettuce leaves for 1 minute until pliable. Use the lettuce to wrap around each trout, leaving the tail visible.

❼ Put the fish in a steamer top, cover tightly and cook for 20 to 25 minutes or until thoroughly cooked. Chop off heads and tails to suit taste. Serve with a lemon or garlic mayonnaise.

This recipe is also delicious using meaty whitefish or rolls of smoked salmon in place of the salmon fillet. Thread chunky vegetables between the fish, such as zucchini, small tomatoes and onions for variety.

SALMON AND WILD MUSHROOM KEBOBS

Serves 4

2 lb (1 kg) salmon fillet or steaks, skinned
8 wild mushrooms, cleaned
1 small yellow bell pepper, cubed
Salt and freshly ground black pepper
Juice and zest of 1 medium lime
1 garlic clove, peeled and crushed
1 Tbsp (15 mL) garlic wine vinegar
2 Tbsp (25 mL) olive oil
1 tsp (5 mL) prepared Dijon mustard
1 Tbsp (15 mL) fresh dill, chopped
¾ cup (150 mL) fish stock
Lime wedges and fresh dill, to garnish
Green salad, to serve

1 Wash the fish under running water and pat dry. Cut into cubes, removing any bones if using steaks. Halve the mushrooms and transfer to a shallow glass dish with the fish and yellow bell pepper. Season well.

2 Mix the lime juice and zest, garlic, vinegar, olive oil, mustard and dill. Pour into the glass dish to coat the ingredients well. Cover and marinate for 2 hours, turning occasionally.

3 Cut four wooden kebob skewers in half. Thread on the fish, bell peppers and mushrooms, alternating ingredients. Reserve marinade.

4 Bring the water in the base of the steamer to a boil. Lay a sheet of foil in the base of the top of the steamer and arrange kebobs inside. Cover with a tight-fitting lid and reduce heat slightly. Cook for 15 minutes.

5 Meanwhile, bring the marinade and stock to a boil in a saucepan until reduced by half. Arrange kebobs on a serving plate and pour the hot marinade over top. Garnish with lime wedges and dill and serve.

Steaming this delicious pasta sauce retains all of the wonderful colors, textures and flavors of the fish and vegetable. Use trout fillets in place of salmon if preferred.

SALMON AND BROCCOLI PENNE

Serves 4

1½ cups (375 mL) dry penne

1 cup (250 mL) broccoli florets

½ Tbsp (7 mL) olive oil

1 tsp (5 mL) garlic wine vinegar

2 garlic cloves, peeled and crushed

Juice and zest of 1 medium orange

12 oz (350 g) salmon fillet, skinned
   and cut into cubes

6 Tbsp (85 mL) dry white wine

¾ cup (150 mL) light cream

2 Tbsp (25 mL) fresh dill, chopped

2 Tbsp (25 mL) freshly grated
   Parmesan cheese

Salt and freshly ground black pepper

Orange wedges and dill, to garnish

❶ Half fill the steamer base with water and bring to a boil. Add the pasta and season with a little salt. Add the pasta a little later according to taste and preference for "doneness."

❷ Place the broccoli in a wax paper-lined steamer tier. Mix the oil, vinegar, garlic, and orange juice and rind together and pour over the broccoli. Rinse the salmon under running water and pat dry. Add the salmon to the pan and cover with a tight-fitting lid.

❸ Set on top of the pasta in salted boiling water for 10 minutes or until the pasta and fish are cooked through.

❹ Meanwhile, heat the wine, cream, dill and Parmesan in a saucepan to just below boiling point. Season to taste.

❺ Drain the pasta and transfer to a warmed serving dish. Spoon the fish and broccoli on top and spoon the sauce over. Garnish, and serve.

Pesto sauce is a terrific partner to salmon, complementing the fish's flavor and color superbly. The sauce may be made 24 hours in advance and stored in the refrigerator.

QUICK FISH WITH PESTO

Serves 4

For the pesto

3 garlic cloves, peeled and chopped

2 Tbsp (25 mL) pine nuts

1 large bunch basil, rinsed

5 Tbsp (65 mL) freshly grated
   Parmesan cheese

1¼ cups (300 mL) extra virgin olive oil

2 Tbsp (25 mL) lemon juice

1 cup (250 mL) dry fusilli

8 steelhead fillets (about 3 oz/75 g each),
   skinned

Salt and freshly ground black pepper

❶ Put the garlic, pine nuts, basil, and Parmesan cheese in a food processor. Gradually blend in the oil with the machine running. Stir in the lemon juice once the sauce is blended.

❷ Meanwhile, bring the water to a boil in the base of the steamer, season with salt and add the pasta. Rinse the fish under cold running water and pat dry. Put the fish fillets in a wax paper-lined steamer top, season with salt and black pepper, cover, and steam for 10 minutes or until the fish is cooked.

❸ Remove the fish and arrange on four serving plates. Spoon the pesto onto the fish and serve with the drained pasta. Garnish with basil.

The colorful relish which accompanies this fish can be stored in the refrigerator; should you have any left over, serve chilled with other fish or meat such as plain pork or chicken.

SALMON WITH CORN RELISH

Serves 4

2 lb (900 g) salmon fillets, cut into equal
   pieces
2 sprigs fresh rosemary
1 garlic clove, peeled
Freshly ground black pepper

For the relish
2 ears of corn
1¼ cups (300 mL) fish stock
1 small red bell pepper, seeded
   and finely chopped
1 small green chile pepper, chopped
2 scallions, chopped
1 Tbsp (15 mL) garlic wine vinegar
1 Tbsp (15 mL) olive oil
2 tsp (10 mL) light brown sugar

1 Wash the fish under running water and pat dry. Arrange with the rosemary and garlic on a sheet of dampened wax paper in the base of the steamer top. Season with pepper.

2 Put the ears of corn, stock, red bell pepper and chile pepper in the base of the steamer and bring to a boil.

3 Put the fish tier on top, cover with a tight-fitting lid and cook for 15 to 20 minutes. Remove the fish and keep warm, discarding the rosemary and garlic.

4 Remove the corn, bell pepper and chile pepper from the stock. Cut the kernels from the corn ears and transfer to a bowl with the chile pepper and bell pepper, scallions, vinegar, oil and sugar.

5 Boil the stock rapidly to reduce by half and add to the corn mixture.

6 Arrange the fish on a warmed serving plate. Garnish with the relish, and serve.

These colorful fish twists are perfect for a dinner party or when you want to impress, without spending hours in the kitchen. They are also a delightful alternative to fish sticks. Plaice is a very versatile, low-fat mild fish. For a lighter version of the sauce, blend ½ cup (90mL) plain yogurt with 1 tsp (5 mL) each of lime and lemon juice and 1 peeled and crushed garlic clove.

FISH BRAIDS WITH LIME SAUCE

Serves 4

1½ lb (650 g) steelhead fillets, skinned
1 lb (450 g) plaice fillets, skinned
Juice and zest of 1 medium lime
1 garlic clove, peeled and crushed

For the sauce
1 cup (250 mL) butter
3 egg yolks
2 Tbsp (25 mL) lime juice
Zest of 1 medium lime
2 garlic cloves, peeled and crushed
2 Tbsp (25 mL) fresh parsley, chopped
Lime wedges and dill, to garnish

❶ Rinse the fillets under running water and pat dry. Cut the steelhead fillets into eight strips and the plaice into four. Trim fish fillets into identical lengths. On a chopping board twist two steelhead fillets around one plaice fillet.

❷ Line a steamer tier with wax paper and place the fish twists in the steamer tier with the lime and garlic.

❸ Cover with a tight-fitting lid and steam over boiling water for 10 minutes or until the fish is cooked through.

❹ After 5 minutes cooking time, begin to make the sauce. Melt the butter in a saucepan. Blend the egg yolks with the lime juice and zest in a food processor and gradually pour in the melted butter with the food processor running. Stir in the garlic and parsley and transfer the sauce to a mixing bowl.

❺ Stand the bowl over a saucepan of hot water while transferring the cooked fish onto warmed plates. Spoon the sauce around the fish, and garnish with lime wedges and dill. Serve immediately.

Marinating the fish in orange, ginger and onion gives it a delicious flavor and keeps it lovely and moist. A colorful and flavorful feast, it may be made with any white fish. A small grapefruit may be used in place of the orange, using only the flesh and not the zest.

ORANGE-GINGER MARINATED WHITEFISH

Serves 4

4 large whitefish fillets, skinned
(about 6 oz/175 g each)
Juice and zest of ½ medium orange
½ in (2.5 cm) piece fresh ginger, grated
2 garlic cloves, crushed
4 scallions, shredded
1 medium orange, segmented
4 Tbsp (50 mL) dry white wine
2 Tbsp (25 mL) butter
1 Tbsp (15 mL) fresh chives, chopped

❶ Rinse the fish under running water and pat dry. Place in a shallow glass dish. Mix half of the orange juice and zest, the ginger, garlic, scallions and half of the orange segments in the dish. Cover and marinate for 1 hour, turning occasionally.

❷ Remove the fish, orange and scallions from the dish, reserving the marinade, and place in a wax paper-lined steamer tier. Cover with a tight-fitting lid and steam for 10 to 15 minutes.

❸ Meanwhile, pour the marinade into a small saucepan with the remaining orange juice, zest and the wine. Bring to a boil and boil rapidly for 2 to 3 minutes to reduce. Remove from the heat. Stir in the butter to give a glossy sauce and add the chives.

❹ Serve the fish on warm plates with the sauce. Garnish with fresh chives and orange segments and serve with freshly steamed rice.

This dish has a Mediterranean flavor, using fresh ripe tomatoes, olives and citrus juice. Served on a croûte of focaccia, it is ideal with a crisp white wine.

COD FOCACCIA

Serves 4

4 cod fillets, skinned
 (about 4 oz/100 g each)
3 Tbsp (45 mL) olive oil
Juice and zest of 2 medium limes
3 garlic cloves, peeled and crushed
1 tsp (5 mL) ground coriander
1 tsp (5 mL) fennel seeds
2 large tomatoes, seeded and cut into eight
4 Tbsp (50 mL) pitted black olives, whole

For the croûte
3 Tbsp (45 mL) butter
1 Tbsp (15 mL) olive oil
4 thick slices focaccia

1 Wash the fish under running water and pat dry. Place in a shallow glass dish. Mix the oil, lime, garlic, coriander and fennel seeds and pour over the fish, turning to coat well. Cover and leave to marinate for at least 1 hour, turning occasionally.

2 Remove the fish from the dish, reserving the marinade, and place in a wax paper-lined steamer tier with the tomatoes and olives. Cover with a tight-fitting lid and steam for 10 to 15 minutes or until the fish is cooked through.

3 Meanwhile, melt the butter with the oil in a skillet. Fry the focaccia in the butter and oil for 2 minutes, turn over, and cook for 2 minutes. Drain on paper towels. Transfer the marinade to a small saucepan and heat through until hot.

4 Top each focaccia with a piece of fish, tomatoes and olives, pour the warm marinade over, and serve with a green salad.

This dish is quite spicy, but the heat can easily be reduced by halving the quantity of chile pepper. The peppers may be prepared up to 24 hours in advance and stored in the refrigerator.

WHITEFISH IN A SPICY PEPPER SAUCE

Serves 4

8 whitefish fillets (about 3 oz/75 g each), skinned
1 Tbsp (15 mL) olive oil
Juice of ½ medium lemon
4 scallions, chopped
2 sprigs fresh basil
Salt and freshly ground black pepper

For the sauce
2 large red bell peppers
1 medium red chile pepper
1¼ cups (300 mL) fish stock
2 Tbsp (25 mL) fresh basil, chopped
Fresh basil leaves, to garnish

❶ Wash the fish under running water and pat dry. Place in a shallow glass dish. Mix the oil, lemon, scallions and basil sprigs, season and pour over the fish. Cover and leave for 2 hours, turning occasionally.

❷ Halve the bell peppers, removing seeds. Place under a hot broiler, skin side uppermost, for 10 minutes. Transfer to a plastic bag, seal and leave for 10 minutes. Remove from the bag and peel.

❸ Finely chop the bell peppers and chile pepper and put in the base of the steamer with the fish stock and chopped basil. Lay a sheet of foil in the steamer top and place the fish fillets and marinade inside. Cover with a tight-fitting lid and steam for 10 minutes over the sauce ingredients.

❹ Remove the fish and scallions from the steamer and keep warm. Transfer the bell peppers and stock to a blender and blend until smooth. Arrange the fish fillets on warmed serving plates. Garnish with the sauce and fresh basil leaves, and serve.

These individual pots may be made with any smoked fish such as cod or salmon for variation. Creamed cottage cheese is used in the recipe, but sifted small-curd cottage cheese will work equally as well.

SMOKED HADDOCK POTS

Serves 4

2 cups (500 mL) fresh spinach, washed and
    stems removed

8 oz (225 g) smoked haddock fillets,
    skinned and flaked

1 egg

1 egg yolk

¾ cup (150 mL) creamed cottage cheese

½ cup (100 mL) plain yogurt

2 Tbsp (25 mL) fresh parsley, chopped

Juice and zest of 1 medium lime

Freshly ground black pepper

1 large tomato, thinly sliced

Lime slices and tomato, to garnish

❶ Prepare the steamer, bringing the water to a boil. Steam the spinach in the top of the steamer for 2 minutes. Remove, and squeeze out any moisture.

❷ Rinse the fish under running water and pat dry. Place with the egg, egg yolk, cheese, yogurt, parsley, lime juice and zest and pepper in a food processor and blend for 30 seconds.

❸ Arrange half of the spinach in the base of four lightly buttered ramekin dishes and top with half of the fish mixture.

❹ Layer the tomatoes on top, and then the remaining fish mixture. Top with the remaining spinach.

❺ Place the dishes in the top of the steamer, cover with a tight-fitting lid and steam for 20 minutes until set. Invert the ramekins onto serving plates, garnish and serve with hot or toasted bread.

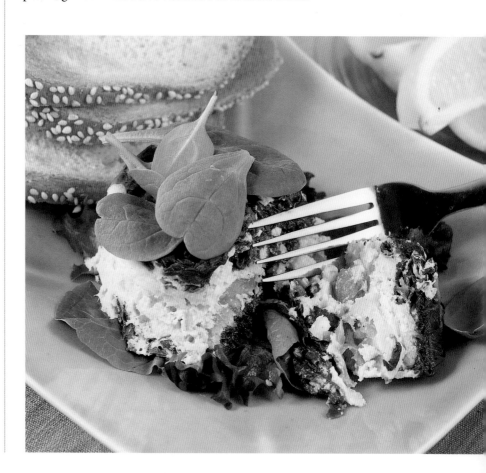

Skate is a wonderful-looking and tasting fish, but if unavailable, use meaty cod or monkfish in its place. Tarragon and fish are a perfect combination, but dill or fennel tops may be used instead for an equally good sauce.

SKATE WITH TARRAGON BUTTER

Serves 4

2 medium-size skate wings,
  about 2 lb (900 g)
³/₄ cup (150 mL) dry vermouth
Juice and zest of 1 medium orange
1 small leek, medium sliced
1 medium red onion, quartered
  and thinly sliced

For the tarragon butter
¹/₂ cup (100 mL) butter
2 Tbsp (25 mL) fresh tarragon, chopped
Few drops of Tabasco Sauce
2 tsp (10 mL) mixed peppercorns,
  partly crushed
Salt
Tarragon sprigs, to garnish

1 Rinse the skate under cold water and pat dry with paper towels. Cut the skate wings in half to give four equal portions.

2 Line two steamer tiers with wax paper and place two portions of fish in each.

3 Mix the vermouth, half of the orange juice and zest and pour over the fish. Add half of the leek and onion to each tier and stack on top of each other in the steamer base. Cover with a tight-fitting lid and cook for 20 minutes, swapping the tiers over halfway through cooking, until the fish is cooked through.

4 Meanwhile, melt the butter in a small saucepan and add the remaining orange juice and zest. Stir in the remaining sauce ingredients and heat gently for 2 to 3 minutes.

5 Remove the skate from the steamer and transfer to warmed serving plates. Spoon the butter over the skate, garnish with orange slices and fresh tarragon sprigs, and serve with freshly steamed vegetables including new potatoes.

Crêpes are a great way to serve fish for a light meal. Make the crêpes up to 24 hours in advance and warm them in the top of the steamer for a few minutes before filling. Crêpes may also be cooked and frozen. Simply defrost at room temperature before you fill them.

SEAFOOD CREPES

Serves 4

For the filling

4 oz (100 g) whitefish fillets

4 oz (100 g) smoked cod fillet

8 oz (225 g) mixed seafood, prepared, such as shelled clams, mussels, squid and peeled and deveined shrimp

3 Tbsp (45 mL) butter

3 Tbsp (45 mL) flour

1¼ cup (300 mL) milk

¾ cup (150 mL) dry white wine

2 Tbsp (25 mL) fresh chives, chopped

1 Tbsp (15 mL) fresh tarragon, chopped

¼ cup (50 mL) freshly grated Cheddar cheese

For the crêpes

½ cup (100 mL) all-purpose flour

Pinch of salt

1 egg

1¼ cup (300 mL) milk

Oil for frying

1 Wash the fish and seafood mixture under cold running water and pat dry. Cut the fish into 1-inch (2.5 cm) cubes. Put the fish and seafood in the top of a wax paper-lined steamer, cover with a tight-fitting lid and steam over boiling water for 5 to 7 minutes until the fish is cooked through.

2 Meanwhile, melt the butter for the sauce and stir in the flour. Cook for 1 minute. Gradually stir in the milk and wine, and bring to a boil, stirring continuously until thickened.

3 Remove the sauce from the heat and stir in the fish and seafood, herbs, and cheese.

4 Sift the flour for the crêpes into a mixing bowl with the salt. Make a well in the center and gradually whisk in the egg and milk to make a smooth batter. Heat a little oil in a 6-inch (15 cm) crêpe pan, pour off into a dish and add a quarter of the batter, turning the pan to coat the base. Cook for 2 minutes and turn the crêpe. Cook for 1 minute and remove. Repeat with the remaining batter, heating oil in the pan for each crêpe.

5 Roll the crêpes into cones and spoon the fish mixture into the center. Arrange on a heatproof plate and put in the top of a prepared steamer. Cover and cook for 5 minutes. Serve immediately with lemon wedges and salad.

If lobster is unavailable or beyond your budget, use cooked shrimp in its place for an equally impressive salad. Serve with warm cheese or garlic bread.

HOT LOBSTER SALAD

Serves 4

Two 1-lb (450 g) cooked lobsters
2 celery ribs, cut into julienne strips
1 medium red onion, halved and finely
   shredded
4 cobs baby corn, halved lengthwise
1 medium carrot, cut into julienne strips
¼ cup (50 mL) snow peas, sliced
Mixed salad greens
Lime quarters, to garnish

For the dressing
2 Tbsp (25 mL) olive oil
1 Tbsp (15 mL) lime juice
1 Tbsp (15 mL) garlic wine vinegar
1 tsp (5 mL) prepared Dijon mustard
2 garlic cloves, peeled and crushed
1 Tbsp (15 mL) fresh dill, chopped

❶ Halve the lobsters and remove the meat. Cut into 1-inch (2.5 cm) cubes. Lay a sheet of dampened wax paper in the base of the steamer top and arrange the lobster and vegetables inside. Cover with a tight-fitting lid and steam over boiling water for 10 minutes until the vegetables are tender and the lobster is hot.

❷ Meanwhile, arrange the salad greens in a shallow serving bowl. Mix the dressing ingredients in a small saucepan and heat gently until hot.

❸ Spoon the lobster and vegetables onto the salad leaves and pour the dressing over the top. Garnish with dill and serve immediately.

Spicy crab makes a great filling for zucchini or other vegetables such as bell peppers and vegetable marrow. Use canned crab meat if fresh is unavailable.

SPICY CRAB-FILLED ZUCCHINI

Serves 4

4 large zucchini

1 small yellow bell pepper, seeded and finely chopped

2 celery ribs, finely chopped

1 Tbsp (15 mL) capers

1 Tbsp (15 mL) pitted black olives, chopped

1 lb (450 g) crab meat

4 Tbsp (50 mL) mayonnaise

1 Tbsp (15 mL) lime juice

Zest of 1 medium lime

Few drops of Tabasco or other hot sauce

Salt and freshly ground black pepper

Pinch of cayenne pepper

¼ cup (50 mL) freshly grated mozzarella cheese

❶ Trim the ends from the zucchini and blanch whole in boiling water for 7 to 8 minutes. Drain well and leave to cool.

❷ Cut zucchinis in half lengthwise and scoop out the seeds with a teaspoon.

❸ Mix the remaining ingredients, except the mozzarella, together and spoon into the zucchini shells. Sprinkle the cheese on top.

❹ Transfer the filled zucchini to a steamer tier, cover with a tight-fitting lid, and steam for 15 to 20 minutes or until hot and cooked through. Serve immediately with a crisp salad. For a crispy filling finish off under the grill.

Steaming is a great way to cook squid as it gives a tender texture. Don't skimp on the marinating time, because the ingredients will soak up the Mediterranean flavors for a fuller taste.

MEDITERRANEAN SQUID

Serves 4

8 large squid, cleaned

1 small red onion, cut into eight

16 black olives, pitted

2 large beefsteak tomatoes,
seeded and chopped

½ cup (100 mL) feta cheese, cubed

2 Tbsp (25 mL) fresh cilantro or
oregano, chopped

For the marinade

2 Tbsp (25 mL) olive oil

2 Tbsp (25 mL) lemon juice

1 garlic clove, peeled and crushed

Freshly ground black pepper

For the sauce

1¼ cups (300 mL) Greek-style yogurt

¼ cup (50 mL) cucumber, finely diced

2 garlic cloves, peeled and crushed

2 tsp (10 mL) lemon juice

Fresh oregano, chopped

Lemon zest, to garnish

❶ Wash the squid under running water and pat dry. Cut into rings. Put in a shallow glass dish with the onion, olives, tomatoes, feta cheese and herbs.

❷ Mix the marinade ingredients and pour over the squid mixture, turning to coat well. Cover and marinate for 1 hour, turning occasionally.

❸ Remove the ingredients from the marinade and arrange on a dampened sheet of wax paper in the base of the steamer top. Bring the water to a boil in the base of the steamer and place the squid and remaining ingredients on top. Cover with a tight-fitting lid and cook for 5 minutes until the squid is tender.

❹ Meanwhile, mix the sauce ingredients together in a bowl and chill.

❺ Serve the squid with warm bread and the dressing on the side.

Fennel is a great accompaniment to succulent mussels, adding a subtle aniseed flavor that is perfect with seafood. Use white grape juice in place of wine as a non-alcoholic variation.

STEAMED MUSSELS WITH CREAMY FENNEL SAUCE

Serves 4

4 lb (2 kg) mussels, scrubbed,
   beards removed
1 small carrot, cut into julienne strips
1 small fennel bulb
2 garlic cloves, peeled and crushed
2½ cups (600 mL) fish stock

For the sauce
2 Tbsp (25 mL) butter
1 small red onion, finely diced
1 garlic clove, peeled and crushed
¼ cup (85 mL) dry white wine
1 Tbsp (15 mL) fresh mixed herbs, chopped
Freshly ground black pepper
¼ cup (85 mL) heavy cream

1 Clean the mussels, removing the beards, and discarding any shells that open when tapped. Place the mussels in the base of the steamer with the carrot strips.

2 Finely shred half of the fennel and add to the pan with the garlic and stock. Cover with a tight-fitting lid and steam for 5 minutes.

3 Discard any unopened mussels and remove all the mussels and vegetables from the stock with a slotted spoon. Keep warm. Measure up ¾ cup of the stock and set aside.

4 Meanwhile, melt the butter in a saucepan and sauté the onion and garlic for 2 minutes until softened. Add the wine, herbs, black pepper and cream. Pour in the ¾ cup (175 mL) of fish stock.

5 Finely chop the remaining fennel and add to the pan. Bring to a boil and cook for 8 to 10 minutes.

6 Spoon the mussels into warmed serving dishes and top with the vegetables. Serve with the wine and cream sauce.

Scallops are delicious with a mild creamy sauce, which enhances but does not overpower their flavor. Steaming scallops ensures that they have a perfect texture and are not overcooked.

SCALLOPS IN SAFFRON CREAM

Serves 4

20 fresh, prepared scallops
Juice and zest of 1 medium lemon
1 garlic clove, peeled and crushed
1 tsp (5 mL) fresh ginger, grated

For the sauce
¾ cup (150 mL) heavy cream
4 Tbsp (50 mL) dry white wine
4 Tbsp (50 mL) fish stock
1 Tbsp (15 mL) fresh chives, chopped
Few saffron strands

1 Rinse the scallops under running water and pat dry. Place in a shallow glass dish. Mix the lemon juice and zest, garlic and ginger, and pour over the scallops. Stir to coat, cover and marinate for 1 hour, turning occasionally.

2 Remove the scallops from the marinade and transfer to a wax paper-lined steamer tier. Cover and steam for 3 to 4 minutes until the scallops are cooked through.

3 Meanwhile, heat the sauce ingredients in a small saucepan and cook for 5 to 7 minutes.

4 Spoon the scallops onto warmed serving plates and serve with the sauce, fresh steamed vegetables and rice or noodles.

The silky sweetness of coconut milk combines with the fiery spices to make this shrimp dish a perfect dinner party recipe. Reduce the quantity of chile used for a milder dish or simply remove the seeds, where most of the "heat" is found.

SPICY GARLIC SHRIMP

Serves 4

10 oz (300 g) uncooked shrimp, peeled and deveined

2 large zucchini, cut into julienne strips

1 medium red chile pepper, finely chopped

1 medium carrot, cut into julienne strips

1 medium red bell pepper, cut into julienne strips

2 medium tomatoes, seeded and chopped

2 Tbsp (25 mL) olive oil

1 tsp (5 mL) fresh ginger, grated

4 garlic cloves, peeled and crushed

Juice and zest of 1 medium lime

1 tsp (5 mL) ground turmeric

1 tsp (5 mL) ground coriander

1 tsp (5 mL) ground cumin

4 Tbsp (50 mL) coconut milk

1 Tbsp (15 mL) light soy sauce

1 cup (250 mL) dry egg noodles

2 Tbsp (25 mL) fresh cilantro, chopped

Fresh cilantro leaves, to garnish

❶ Rinse the shrimp under running water and pat dry. Put in a shallow glass dish with the vegetables. Mix the oil, ginger, garlic, lime, spices, coconut milk and soy sauce together, and pour over the ingredients. Stir to coat, cover and marinate for 1 hour, turning occasionally.

❷ Half-fill the base of the steamer with water and bring to a boil. Cover the base of the steamer top with dampened wax paper and add the shrimp, vegetables and marinade. Place over the steamer base, cover with a tight-fitting lid and steam for 10 minutes. Put the noodles into the boiling water in the steamer base. Replace the shrimp and cook for a further 5 minutes or until the noodles and shrimp are cooked.

❸ Remove the steamer top and drain the noodles. Arrange on a warmed serving plate and top with the shrimp mixture. Garnish with chopped cilantro, and serve.

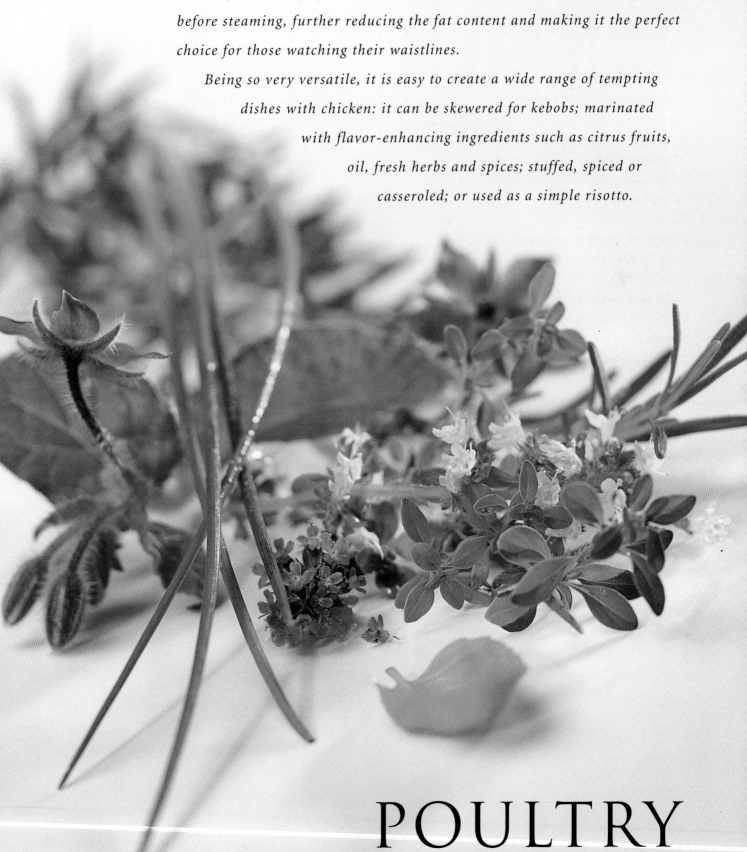

*S*teaming is an excellent way to preserve the moist goodness and flavor of poultry. All poultry is a good source of protein, vitamins and minerals and is one of the most popular meats in our diet. Most of the poultry is skinned before steaming, further reducing the fat content and making it the perfect choice for those watching their waistlines.

Being so very versatile, it is easy to create a wide range of tempting dishes with chicken: it can be skewered for kebobs; marinated with flavor-enhancing ingredients such as citrus fruits, oil, fresh herbs and spices; stuffed, spiced or casseroled; or used as a simple risotto.

POULTRY

The caramelized pineapple gives this colorful dish a real look and taste of the Caribbean, and complements the spicy chicken perfectly.

CARIBBEAN CHICKEN

Serves 4

4 chicken breast fillets (4 oz/100 g each),
   skinned
Salt and freshly ground black pepper
Juice and zest of 1 medium lime
1 Tbsp (15 mL) olive oil
1 medium red onion, halved and thinly sliced
4 garlic cloves, peeled and crushed
2 tsp (10 mL) fresh ginger, grated
1 medium red chile pepper, chopped
2 large tomatoes, seeded and chopped
1 cup (250 mL) sweet potato,
   peeled and chopped
1 medium ripe plantain, chopped
2½ cups (600 mL) chicken stock
1 cinnamon stick
1 cup (250 mL) rice
2 Tbsp (25 mL) butter
2 Tbsp (25 mL) light brown sugar
1 small pineapple, cored and
   cut into 16 wedges
Fresh parsley, chopped, to garnish

❶ Rinse the chicken under cold water and pat dry. Season with salt and pepper and roll in the lime juice and zest.

❷ Heat the oil in the base of the steamer and sauté the chicken for 3 to 4 minutes, turning until sealed. Add the onion, garlic, ginger and chile pepper, and cook for a further 2 minutes.

❸ Stir in the tomatoes, sweet potato and plantain. Add the stock and cinnamon, cover, and cook 1 hour.

❹ Meanwhile, boil the rice for 15 minutes and drain well. Line the steamer top with a clean damp dish towel and spoon in the rice. Cover with the lid and cook over the chicken mixture for 15 minutes until cooked through.

❺ Melt the butter in a skillet with the sugar and add the pineapple. Cook for 5 minutes, turning until hot and coated in syrup. Be careful not to burn.

❻ Spoon the rice onto a warm serving plate and top with the chicken mixture. Serve with the hot pineapple and garnish with parsley.

This dish has quite a delicate flavor. Serve with steamed rice and vegetables for a refreshing summer meal. Mango chunks would be ideal in place of grapes.

GARLIC CHICKEN WITH CUCUMBER AND GRAPES

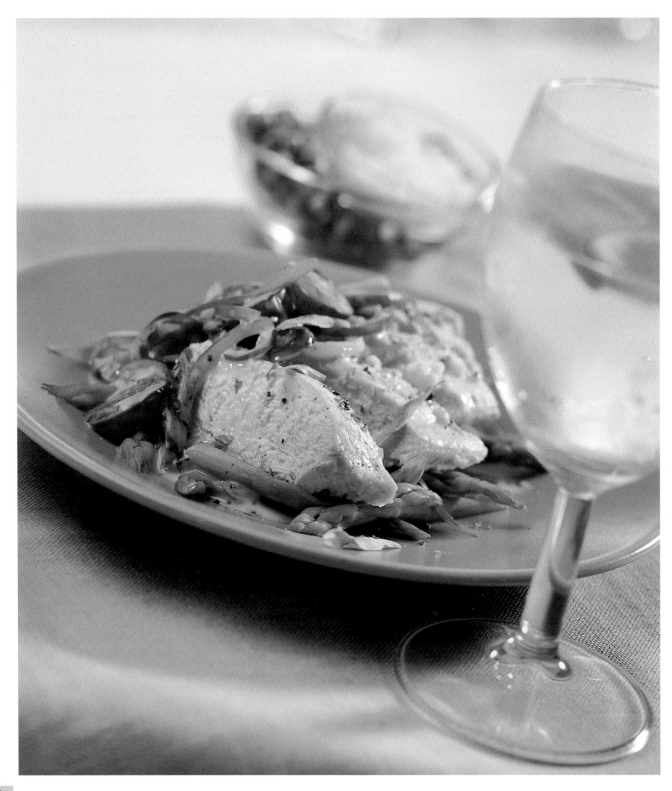

Serves 4

4 skinned chicken breasts
  (about 4 oz/100 g each)
1 garlic clove
Salt and freshly ground black pepper
1 medium cucumber, cut into julienne strips
½ cup (100 mL) seedless red grapes, halved

For the sauce
¾ cup (150 mL) chicken stock
6 Tbsp (75 mL) light cream
2 Tbsp (25 mL) fresh tarragon, chopped
1 egg yolk

❶ Rinse the chicken breasts under cold water and pat dry. Rub the garlic over both sides, season with salt and pepper and place in the bottom tier of the steamer with the garlic.

❷ Steam for 15 minutes.

❸ Place the cucumber and grapes in the second steamer tier over the chicken and cook both tiers for 5 minutes or until chicken is cooked.

❹ Meanwhile, mix all of the sauce ingredients, except the egg, in a small saucepan and heat gently, but do not boil. Remove from the heat and whisk in the egg.

❺ Remove the cucumber and grapes from the steamer and stir into the sauce. Transfer the chicken to warmed serving plates and serve with the sauce and fresh steamed vegetables.

This is a richly warming winter dish, and with its potato topping, a meal in itself. Drier than a traditional hot pot, it is also ideal made with lamb chops.

CHICKEN HOT POT

Serves 4

4 chicken pieces, deboned, skinned and
  halved (about 10 oz/300 g each)
2 medium carrots, thinly sliced
2 celery ribs, finely chopped
1 cup (250 mL) rutabaga, roughly chopped
1 medium red onion, quartered
  and thinly sliced
4 Tbsp (50 mL) green beans, cut into thirds
4 Tbsp (50 mL) baby corn, halved lengthwise
2 Tbsp (25 mL) fresh thyme, chopped
1 bay leaf
¾ cup (150 mL) chicken stock
6 Tbsp (85 mL) dry cider or apple juice
Salt and freshly ground black pepper
2 large potatoes, peeled and scrubbed

❶ Rinse the chicken pieces under running water and pat dry. Put with the vegetables, herbs, stock, and cider or apple juice in a heatproof dish which fits in the steamer top. Season well.

❷ Cover tightly with pleated foil and secure with string.

❸ Put the potatoes in salted boiling water in the base of the steamer, place the chicken mixture tier on top, cover tightly, and steam for 1 to 1½ hours or until cooked through.

❹ Remove the potatoes from the water after 10 minutes and slice thin. Arrange on dampened wax paper in the upper steamer tier and steam over the chicken for 20 minutes, or until tender.

❺ Remove the potatoes and chicken from the steamer. Spoon the chicken and vegetables onto warmed serving plates and top with sliced potato. Serve with a fresh green salad and crusty bread.

Making a risotto in the base of a steamer means that the two tiers may be used to cook a first course and dessert at the same time. Be sure to use arborio rice, now widely available.

CHICKEN AND SAFFRON RISOTTO WITH LEEKS AND ASPARAGUS

Serves 4

4 Tbsp (50 mL) butter

2 medium leeks, finely chopped

2 garlic cloves, peeled and crushed

1 medium red bell pepper, diced

1 cup (250 mL) arborio rice

1 lb (450 g) lean chicken, diced,
   skinned and deboned

Few saffron strands

2 cups (450 mL) chicken stock

¾ cup (150 mL) dry white wine

8 baby corn, halved lengthwise

4 Tbsp (50 mL) frozen peas

Salt and freshly ground black pepper

4 Tbsp (50 mL) asparagus spears,
   cut into quarters

4 Tbsp (50 mL) freshly grated
   Parmesan cheese

❶ Melt the butter in the base of a steamer. Sauté the leek, garlic and bell pepper for 2 to 3 minutes, stirring. Add rice. Cook for 2 minutes.

❷ Rinse the chicken under running water and pat dry. Stir with the saffron into the pan. Mix the stock and wine together and pour in a third of the quantity. Bring to a boil, reduce to simmer, and cover with a tight-fitting lid for 20 minutes.

❸ Stir in the corn and peas, season, and add another third of the liquid. Cover again and cook for a further 20 minutes.

❹ Add the remaining liquid, the asparagus and cheese, cover and cook for 10 minutes, or until the rice is tender. Serve immediately.

Traditionally cooked in a large, shallow open skillet and in large quantities, paella is the flagship of Spanish cooking. By using your covered steamer base to cook the following variation, all of the aromatic flavors contained within the recipe are retained and the textures of the rice and vegetables are perfect. If saffron is unavailable, use ½ tsp (3 mL) of turmeric in its place for color.

PAELLA

Serves 4

1 lb (450 g) boneless, skinned
   chicken, cubed
2 Tbsp (25 mL) olive oil
4 slices salami
1 large red onion, quartered and thinly sliced
2 garlic cloves, peeled and crushed
1 large red bell pepper, cubed
¾ cup (150 mL) arborio rice
2½ cups (600 mL) chicken stock
Salt and freshly ground black pepper
Large pinch of cayenne pepper
Few saffron strands
½ cup (100 mL) peeled, deveined shrimp
16 mussels, scrubbed, beards removed
¼ cup (50 mL) peas
Fresh parsley, chopped, to garnish

❶ Rinse the chicken under running water and pat dry. Heat the oil in the base of the steamer and cook the chicken for 3 to 4 minutes, turning until browned. Add the salami, onion, garlic, bell pepper and rice, and cook for a further 5 minutes, stirring.

❷ Add the stock and season with salt and pepper. Add the cayenne and saffron, cover, and steam over a gentle heat for 15 minutes.

❸ Add the remaining ingredients, replace the lid, and cook for a further 5 to 7 minutes until the chicken and rice are cooked through.

❹ Spoon into a warmed serving dish and garnish with chopped parsley.

Pecans and blue cheese are a great combination and make for a wonderful sauce with these colorful moist chicken pockets. Walnuts could be used in place of pecans or macadamia nuts.

STUFFED CHICKEN IN A BLUE CHEESE AND PECAN SAUCE

Serves 4

4 chicken escalopes (about 4 oz/100 g each)

Salt and freshly ground black pepper

4 Tbsp (50 mL) fresh whole wheat bread crumbs

2 Tbsp (25 mL) pecans, chopped

5 scallions, finely chopped

2 garlic cloves, peeled and crushed

1 small red bell pepper, finely chopped

2 tsp (10 mL) lemon juice

Zest of 1 medium lemon

2 Tbsp (25 mL) butter, melted

For the sauce

1 Tbsp (15 mL) butter

1 Tbsp (15 mL) all-purpose flour

¾ cup (150 mL) milk

6 Tbsp (75 mL) dry white wine

4 Tbsp (50 mL) soft blue cheese, crumbled

2 Tbsp (25 mL) pecans, chopped

4 Tbsp (50 mL) fresh watercress, chopped

4 Tbsp (50 mL) plain yogurt

Lemon wedges and watercress, to garnish

❶ Rinse the chicken under running water and pat dry. Place between two sheets of wax paper and beat with a mallet until ¼-inch (6 mm) in thickness. Be careful not to pound too thin. Cut a slit in the side of each escalope to form a pocket. Season the inside of the pocket with salt and pepper.

❷ Mix the remaining stuffing ingredients together and spoon into the pockets, pressing in with the back of a spoon.

❸ Put the chicken pieces in the top of a steamer lined with damp wax paper. Cover and steam for 15 minutes until the chicken is cooked through.

❹ Meanwhile, melt the butter for the sauce in a pan and add the flour. Cook for 1 minute and gradually stir in the milk and wine. Bring to a boil until the sauce thickens.

❺ Add the cheese, pecans, watercress, and yogurt, and heat gently until the cheese has melted.

❻ Remove the chicken from the steamer and place on a warmed serving plate. Spoon on the sauce and serve garnished with lemon and watercress.

Couscous is granular semolina which cooks up light and fluffy. Steaming is the best method of cooking the grain, which is enhanced by the addition of butter to separate the grains after cooking.

CHICKEN COUSCOUS

Serves 4

2¼ lb (1 kg) lean boneless chicken, cubed, skinned
1 Tbsp (15 mL) olive oil
4 cups (1 L) chicken stock
1 large red onion, cut into eight
2 garlic cloves, chopped
Pinch of saffron strands
½ cinnamon stick, bruised
4 medium tomatoes, seeded and quartered
2 large carrots, cut into chunks
½ large turnip, cut into eight
2 medium zucchini, thickly sliced
2 Tbsp (25 mL) raisins
1 tsp (5 mL) ground coriander
Large pinch cayenne pepper
Salt and freshly ground black pepper
1½ cups (350 mL) couscous
2 Tbsp (25 mL) butter
Cilantro sprigs, to garnish

❶ Rinse the chicken under running water and pat dry. Heat the oil in the steamer base and sauté the chicken, onion and garlic for 3 to 4 minutes until the chicken is sealed. Pour in chicken stock to just cover the meat and add the saffron, cinnamon, tomatoes, carrots, turnips, zucchini, raisins, coriander and cayenne. Season well, cover with a tight-fitting lid, and steam for 1¼ hours until the meat is tender and cooked through.

❷ Meanwhile, soak the couscous in a bowl of cold water for 20 minutes, 50 minutes before the meat is done. Drain well. Line the steamer top with a clean, damp dish towel and spoon in the couscous. Cover with the lid and place over the meat and vegetables in the base of the steamer. Steam for 30 minutes until the couscous is cooked through.

❸ Stir the butter into the couscous and separate with a fork to remove any lumps. Spoon onto a warmed serving plate and spoon the meat mixture on top. Garnish and serve.

Make these great chicken rolls in advance and store in the refrigerator for up to 4 hours, ready to cook, for a fast but impressive meal. Reheat by steaming for 7 to 10 minutes.

HERB AND MUSHROOM CHICKEN ROLLS

Serves 4

4 boneless chicken breasts, skinned
  (about 4 oz/100 g each)
Salt and freshly ground black pepper
¼ cup (50 mL) mushrooms,
  cleaned and chopped
2 scallions, chopped
2 garlic cloves, peeled and crushed
1 small red bell pepper, finely chopped
6 Tbsp (75 mL) cream cheese
4 Tbsp (50 mL) cooked rice, preferably mix of
  wild and long-grain rice

For the butter
6 Tbsp (75 mL) butter
2 garlic cloves, crushed
2 Tbsp (25 mL) fresh tarragon, chopped
1 Tbsp (15 mL) fresh parsley, chopped

❶ Rinse the chicken under running water and pat dry. Place between two sheets of wax paper and beat with a mallet or rolling pin until ¼-inch (6 mm) thick. Season.

❷ Mix together the mushrooms, scallions, garlic, bell pepper and cream cheese. Stir in the rice. Spoon the filling along the length of the chicken and roll up. Secure with a toothpick and place in a steamer tier.

❸ Place the butter, garlic, and herbs in a small heatproof bowl which fits the steamer tier, and set aside.

❹ Cover the chicken with a tight-fitting lid and steam for 20 minutes or until the chicken is cooked through.

❺ Five minutes before the chicken is cooked, place the butter mixture in its bowl, into a tier over the chicken, cover, and steam until melted and hot.

❻ Transfer the chicken to warmed serving plates and spoon the butter over the top. Serve immediately.

Wrapping the marinated chicken pieces in basil leaves adds great color and flavor. Baby spinach or sorrel could be used in its place to create the perfect light and tasty summer dish.

BASIL-WRAPPED MARINATED CHICKEN KEBOBS

Serves 4

12 oz (350 g) boneless chicken, skinned
4 Tbsp (50 mL) walnut oil
1 Tbsp (15 mL) balsamic vinegar
Juice of ½ medium orange
2 Tbsp (25 mL) liquid honey
1 large bunch fresh basil
1 shallot, chopped
1 medium yellow bell pepper, cubed
12 button mushrooms, cleaned
12 medium cherry tomatoes
1 medium head chicory or heart
  of 1 small lettuce
Oak leaf lettuce

For the dressing
2 Tbsp (25 mL) walnut oil
2 Tbsp (25 mL) garlic wine vinegar
1 tsp (5 mL) prepared mustard
2 Tbsp (25 mL) liquid honey
Juice of ½ medium orange
Salt and freshly ground black pepper

❶ Rinse the chicken under running water and pat dry. Cut into 1-inch (2.5 cm) cubes and put in a shallow glass dish. Mix the walnut oil, vinegar, orange juice, honey, a few basil leaves and the shallot, and pour over the chicken, turning to coat. Cover, and leave to marinate for 1 hour, turning occasionally.

❷ Remove the chicken from the marinade and wrap each piece in a basil leaf. Thread onto four halved, wooden skewers with the bell pepper, mushrooms and cherry tomatoes. Arrange on a heatproof plate in the base of the steamer top, cover with a tight-fitting lid, and steam for 15 minutes until the chicken is cooked through.

❸ Meanwhile, mix the dressing ingredients in a small saucepan and gently heat. Arrange the salad leaves on a serving plate and place the cooked kebobs on top.

❹ Drizzle the warm dressing over and then garnish with freshly ground pepper.

Steaming a whole chicken is the perfect way to obtain a really succulent result, and helps the meat to take on the wonderful Thai flavorings. If lime leaves are unavailable, use large mint or basil leaves.

WHOLE THAI-SPICED CHICKEN WITH A COCONUT SAUCE

Serves 4

3 lb (1.4 kg) oven-ready chicken

1 large lemon, halved

2 tsp (10 mL) fresh ginger, grated

1 large red chile pepper, finely chopped

2 garlic cloves, peeled and crushed

2 tsp (10 mL) lemongrass, finely chopped

Juice of 1 medium lime

1 Tbsp (15 mL) fresh cilantro, chopped

Salt and freshly ground black pepper

½ tsp (3 mL) Thai spice powder (chile powder, dried garlic, ginger, ground coriander, ground cinnamon, ground cumin, star anise and ground garlic)

2 Tbsp (25 mL) vegetable oil

¾ cup (150 mL) dry white wine

Lime leaves

For the sauce

¾ cup (150 mL) chicken stock

¾ cup (150 mL) coconut milk

❶ Wash the chicken inside and out, and pat dry. Place the halved lemon inside the cavity and transfer to a deep glass dish.

❷ Mix the remaining marinade ingredients together (except the lime leaves) and pour over the chicken. Cover tightly and leave to marinate for at least 2 hours, turning occasionally.

❸ Prepare the steamer, lining the base of the upper tier with the lime leaves. Remove the chicken from the dish, reserving the marinade, and place on top of the lime leaves. Cover and steam for 1 to 1¼ hours until cooked through.

❹ Meanwhile, heat the marinade in a small saucepan with the stock and coconut milk. Serve with the chicken and jasmine rice.

Your butcher, or the gourmet meat section at a well-stocked supermarket, should have poussin, which are small, very young chickens. If unavailable, use small chicken pieces or quarters.

POUSSIN WITH CHILE NECTARINES

Serves 4

4 poussins (about 12 oz/350 g each)

For the marinade
2 garlic cloves, peeled and crushed
1 red chile pepper, chopped
1 shallot, finely chopped
4 Tbsp (50 mL) olive oil
1 Tbsp (15 mL) balsamic vinegar

For the sauce
2 Tbsp (25 mL) butter
2 large ripe nectarines, chopped
    into medium chunks
1 medium red chile pepper, finely chopped
2 scallions, chopped
3 Tbsp (45 mL) dry sherry
1 cup (250 mL) chicken stock

Ripe nectarines, orange and chile pepper,
    for garnish
Fresh watercress, to garnish

❶ Rinse the poussin under running water and pat dry. Cut down each side of the backbone, and remove the bone (or ask your butcher to do). Lay the birds breast side down on a chopping board and press down to flatten them out.

❷ Lay the birds in a shallow glass dish, mix the marinade ingredients together, and pour over the birds, turning to coat. Cover and leave to marinate for 1 hour, turning occasionally.

❸ Remove the poussins and lay them in the base of the steamer top on a sheet of dampened wax paper. Cover and steam for 25 minutes or until cooked through.

❹ Meanwhile, for the sauce, melt the butter in a small pan and add the remaining sauce ingredients. Bring to a boil, reduce the heat to simmer, and cook for 10 minutes.

❺ Remove the poussins from the steamer and place on a warm serving dish. Spoon the sauce over, garnish, and serve with boiled potatoes.

There are many ready-to-eat dried fruits available which add to this dish's intense flavor. Choose a wide mixture such as pears, mango, apple, sultana raisins or cherries for best results.

CHICKEN WITH SPICY DRIED FRUIT

Serves 4

12 chicken wings (about 3 oz/75 g each)
¾ cup (150 mL) mixed dried fruits, such as apricots, prunes, sultana raisins, peaches, roughly chopped
2 Tbsp (25 mL) dry sherry
6 Tbsp (75 mL) orange juice
1 tsp (5 mL) ground coriander
½ tsp (3 mL) ground cumin
½ tsp (3 mL) ground cinnamon
½ tsp (3 mL) chile powder
2 garlic cloves, peeled and crushed
2 Tbsp (25 mL) liquid honey
2 Tbsp (25 mL) butter

For the rice
6 Tbsp (75 mL) long-grain rice
2½ cups (600 mL) chicken stock
2 scallions, chopped
Pinch of turmeric
1 small red chile pepper, chopped
Orange segments, to garnish

1 Rinse the chicken under running water and pat dry. Place in a shallow glass dish with the fruit, sherry, orange juice, spices, garlic and honey. Cover and leave to marinate for 1 hour, turning occasionally.

2 Meanwhile, cook the rice in the stock with the scallions, turmeric and chile pepper in the base of the steamer for 15 minutes. Drain well and spoon into four ramekins or molds.

3 Remove the chicken from the dish, reserving the marinade, and place in the bottom tier of the steamer. Put the rice molds in the next tier and place on top. Cover with a tight-fitting lid and steam for 20 minutes or until the chicken is cooked through.

4 Meanwhile, heat the marinade in a small saucepan and whisk in the butter to give a glossy sauce.

5 Transfer the chicken to warm plates; spoon the sauce over.

Turn a rice mold onto each plate and garnish with orange segments. Serve immediately.

*The poussin are spiced with paprika and cinnamon,
and served with a rich, gamy sauce. Cornish hens,
quails and even chicken portions can also be used.*

POUSSIN WITH SPICY RAISIN SAUCE

Serves 4

2 poussins of equal size, halved
   (about 12-15 oz/350-450 g each)
Juice of 1 large lime
1 tsp (5 mL) cinnamon
1 tsp (5 mL) paprika

For the sauce
¾ cup (150 mL) red wine
6 Tbsp (75 mL) chicken stock
3 Tbsp (45 mL) raisins
½ tsp (3 mL) cinnamon
2 Tbsp (25 mL) butter

❶ Rinse the poussin under water and pat dry. Rub with the lime juice, cinnamon and paprika, and place in a steamer tier over boiling water. Cover and cook for 25 minutes or until cooked through.

❷ Meanwhile, place all of the sauce ingredients, except the butter, in a small saucepan and bring to a boil. Boil rapidly to reduce by half.

❸ Whisk the butter into the sauce a little at a time, until sauce is smooth and glossy.

❹ Remove the poussin from the steamer and serve glazed with the sauce.

---

*This dish has a slightly Oriental flavor which perfectly
complements the tender poussin. Serve with steamed
scented rice and/or mixed vegetables.*

POUSSIN WITH ORANGE AND GINGER

Serves 4

4 poussins (about 12 oz/350 g each)
Juice and zest of 2 medium oranges
1 in (2.5 cm) piece ginger, finely shredded
2 garlic cloves, peeled and crushed
2 Tbsp (25 mL) fino sherry
1 Tbsp (15 mL) light soy sauce
Several scallions, shredded
4 Tbsp (50 mL) butter
1 orange, peeled and segmented, to garnish

❶ Rinse the poussin under running water and pat dry. Put in a deep dish. Mix the orange juice and half of the zest, the ginger, garlic, sherry and soy sauce together, and pour over the poussin, turning to coat. Cover and marinate for 1 hour, turning occasionally.

❷ Remove the birds from the dish, reserving the marinade.

❸ Arrange the scallions in the base of the steamer top on a dampened piece of wax paper, add the poussin and cover tightly.

❹ Steam for 30 minutes or until cooked through. Meanwhile, heat the marinade in a small pan and whisk in the butter to make a rich glossy sauce.

❺ Remove the poussin from the steamer and arrange on warmed serving plates. Pour the sauce over, garnish, and serve with rice and/or fresh lightly stir-fried vegetables.

Turkey is a great meat year-round, full of taste and low in fat. In this recipe it takes on a slightly Oriental flavor.

TURKEY KEBOBS WITH ONION RELISH

Serves 4

12 oz (350 g) lean, skinned turkey, cubed

1 Tbsp (15 mL) dark soy sauce

1 Tbsp (15 mL) light soy sauce

2 Tbsp (25 mL) fino sherry

1 medium red chile pepper, finely chopped

2 garlic cloves, peeled and crushed

1 medium zucchini, cut into
   1 in (2.5 cm) chunks

8 artichoke hearts, canned

8 small cherry tomatoes

1 medium lime, cut into quarters

For the relish

2 Tbsp (25 mL) butter

1 Tbsp (15 mL) oil

1 large onion, halved and sliced

¼ cup (75 mL) vegetable stock

1 Tbsp (15 mL) dry sherry

1 tsp (5 mL) cornstarch

1 Tbsp (15 mL) fresh parsley, chopped

Freshly ground black pepper

❶ Rinse the turkey under running water and pat dry. Place in a shallow glass dish with the soy sauces, sherry, chile and garlic. Cover and marinate for 1 hour, turning occasionally.

❷ Thread the turkey and vegetables onto four halved wooden skewers and place in the top of the steamer. Steam for 15 to 20 minutes.

❸ Melt the butter with the oil in a saucepan and fry the onion for 10 minutes until browned. Add all of the remaining ingredients except the cornstarch, cover, and cook for 10 minutes.

❹ Blend the cornstarch with 4 teaspoons (20 mL) cold water and whisk into the relish. Bring to a boil, stirring until thickened and clear. Serve immediately with the kebobs and a green salad.

This is quite a rich dish filled with strong flavors both in the meat and the sauce. Chicken, turkey, or any game bird could be used in place of the duck. Serve with boiled potatoes as a foil against the duck's richness.

MADEIRA DUCK WITH MIXED WILD MUSHROOMS

Serves 4

4 boneless duck breasts (about
   6 oz/175 g each), skinned

3 garlic cloves, peeled and crushed

1¼ cups (300 mL) chicken stock

¼ cup (100 mL) Madeira

4 Tbsp (50 mL) cherry preserves

1 cup (250 mL) mixed mushrooms,
   cleaned and thinly sliced

2 Tbsp (25 mL) fresh parsley, chopped

Salt and freshly ground black pepper

1 Tbsp (15 mL) cornstarch

❶ Rinse the duck under running water and pat dry. Slice the duck breasts and place in a shallow glass dish. Mix one third of the garlic cloves, the stock, Madeira, and preserves together, and spoon over the duck. Cover and marinate for 1 hour, turning occasionally.

❷ Line the steamer top with dampened wax paper and add the mushrooms. Sprinkle with the remaining garlic and the parsley.

❸ Remove the duck breasts from the dish, reserving the marinade, and place on top of the mushrooms. Cover and steam for 40 minutes or until cooked through.

❹ Meanwhile, heat the marinade in a small saucepan. Blend the cornstarch with 2 tablespoons (25 mL) of cold water to make a paste and whisk into the marinade. Bring to a boil, stirring until thickened and clear. Arrange a few mushrooms on each of four serving plates, top with the duck breasts, pour the sauce over, and serve with steamed rice.

Duck is a rich, strong-flavored meat ideal countered by a citrus flavor such as lime. Ginger adds warmth. Any fruit jelly, such as currant, apple or gooseberry may be used in place of the port-and-cranberry jelly. The dish would also be ideal with turkey and chicken.

GINGER-LIME DUCK ON A BED OF SPINACH

Serves 4

4 boneless duck breasts, skinned
   (about 6 oz/175 g each)
4 Tbsp (50 mL) port-and-cranberry jelly
½ cup (100 mL) fresh baby spinach, washed
1 large carrot, cut into julienne strips
2 celery ribs, cut into julienne strips
¼ cup (50 mL) snow peas
1 medium red onion, quartered
   and thinly sliced
2 medium limes
½ in (2.5 cm) piece fresh ginger, grated
2 cups (450 mL) chicken stock
¾ cup (150 mL) red wine
Lime zest and wedges, and parsley, to garnish

❶ Rinse the duck breasts under running water and pat dry. Brush with the jelly, coating both sides, and set aside.

❷ Lay the spinach in the base of a wax paper-lined steamer tier and top with the remaining vegetables, the juice and zest of 1 lime, the ginger, and duck breasts.

❸ Pour the stock and wine into the base of the steamer with the remaining lime juice, and bring to a boil. Place the duck over the stock, cover with a tight-fitting lid, and steam for 25 to 30 minutes until the duck is cooked through.

❹ Remove the duck and vegetables from the steamer and keep warm. Boil the sauce to reduce by half. Serve the duck on the bed of vegetables with the sauce poured over. Garnish and serve. Excellent with rice or small boiled potatoes.

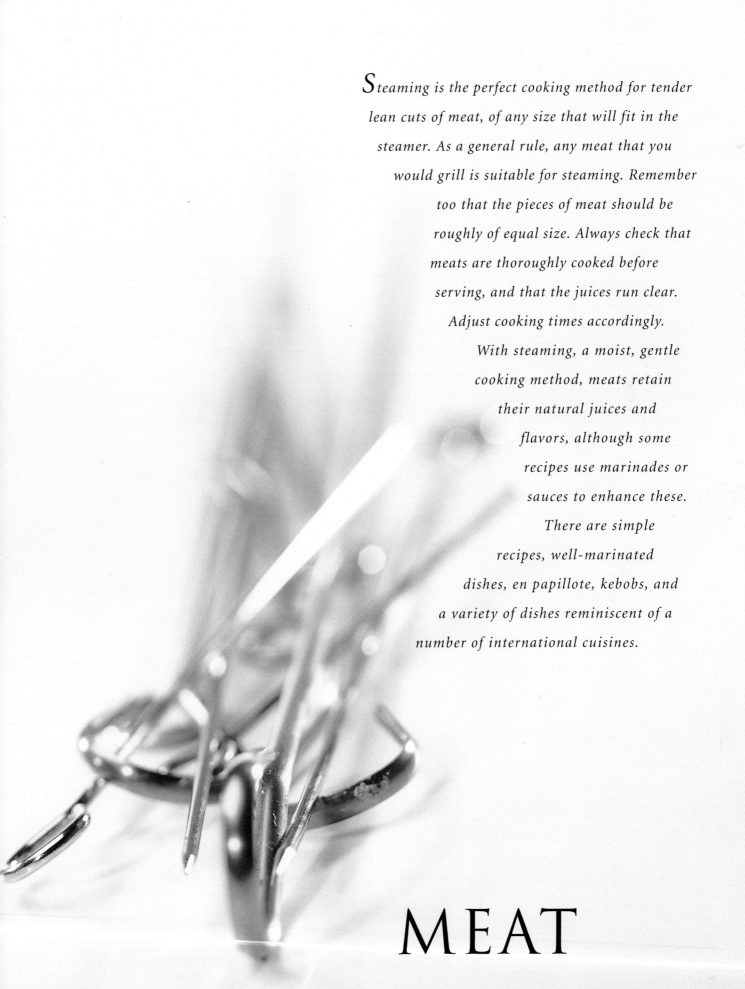

Steaming is the perfect cooking method for tender lean cuts of meat, of any size that will fit in the steamer. As a general rule, any meat that you would grill is suitable for steaming. Remember too that the pieces of meat should be roughly of equal size. Always check that meats are thoroughly cooked before serving, and that the juices run clear. Adjust cooking times accordingly. With steaming, a moist, gentle cooking method, meats retain their natural juices and flavors, although some recipes use marinades or sauces to enhance these. There are simple recipes, well-marinated dishes, en papillote, kebobs, and a variety of dishes reminiscent of a number of international cuisines.

MEAT

A rich marinade gives the pork a tangy, slightly Oriental flavor and makes a lovely glaze for the cooked meat and potatoes. The pork should be sliced across the grain for extra tenderness.

PORK TENDERLOIN WITH POTATO CROUTE

Serves 4

12 oz (350 g) pork fillet, sliced

2 Tbsp (25 mL) dark soy sauce

2 Tbsp (25 mL) liquid honey

1 Tbsp (15 mL) sherry

2 Tbsp (25 mL) orange juice

1 garlic clove, peeled and crushed

2 large potatoes, peeled

1 medium carrot, cut into julienne strips

4 scallions, shredded

Orange wedges, to serve

❶ Cut the pork into thin slices and place in a shallow glass dish. Mix together the soy sauce, honey, sherry, orange juice and garlic, and pour over the pork, turning to coat. Cover and leave to marinate for 2 hours.

❷ Meanwhile, cook the potatoes in boiling salted water in the steamer base for 5 minutes. Remove with a slotted spoon and slice very thinly. On a heatproof plate, arrange the potatoes in four circles, overlapping the slices, and place in the upper steamer tier.

❸ Remove the pork from the marinade and place in the base of the lower steamer tier on dampened wax paper. Top with the carrots and scallions.

❹ Place the pork over the steamer base, followed by the potatoes. Cover with a tight-fitting lid and steam for 25 minutes until the pork and potatoes are cooked through.

❺ Meanwhile, in a separate pan, heat the marinade until reduced to a glossy sauce.

❻ Transfer the potato croûtes to four warm serving plates and top each with pork and vegetables. Spoon the glaze over the top, garnish with orange wedges, and serve with freshly steamed green vegetables.

This recipe uses classic goulash ingredients, but is a drier version —ideal served with mashed or sautéed potatoes. Tender beef or lamb are ideal substitutes for pork, and plain yogurt may be used instead of sour cream.

HUNGARIAN PORK

Serves 4

10 oz (300 g) pork tenderloin, trimmed and thinly sliced

2 Tbsp (25 mL) butter

1 medium onion, cut into eight

2 garlic cloves, peeled and crushed

2 medium carrots, cut into julienne strips

4 large tomatoes, seeded and chopped

4 Tbsp (50 mL) pork or vegetable stock

2 tsp (10 mL) paprika

¾ cup (150 mL) sour cream

2 Tbsp (25 mL) fresh parsley, chopped

❶ Place all of the ingredients, except the sour cream and parsley, in a deep, heatproof bowl which fits into the steamer top. Put in the steamer and cover with a tight-fitting lid.

❷ Steam for 30 minutes until the meat is tender and cooked through.

❸ Add the sour cream and parsley to the bowl, stirring well. Replace the lid, and steam for a further 5 minutes. Serve with mashed or sautéed potatoes, or noodles.

Perfect for a quick family supper, this recipe is delicious made with either cider or apple juice, but be sure to use unsweetened as this will affect the final flavor. Remember to slice pork across the grain for a tender result.

PORK TENDERLOIN WITH CIDER

Serves 4

1 lb (450 g) pork tenderloin,
   trimmed and thinly sliced
2 medium leeks, halved lengthwise and sliced
8 baby corn, halved lengthwise
8 baby carrots, halved lengthwise
¾ cup (150 mL) unsweetened
   apple cider or juice
2 Tbsp (25 mL) fresh sage, chopped
7 Tbsp (85 mL) heavy cream
Salt and freshly ground black pepper

❶ Cut pork into thin slices. Place in center of a large square of foil.

❷ Bring the sides of the foil up and fold to make a parcel, leaving the top open.

❸ Add the leeks, corn and carrots, and pour in the cider. Add the sage and seal the top of the parcel.

❹ Transfer the parcel to a steamer tier, cover with a tight-fitting lid and steam for 15 minutes.

❺ Add the cream to the parcel and season to taste. Cover with the lid and steam for a further 5 minutes or until the pork is cooked through. Serve with rice or mashed potatoes.

This dish makes full use of the steamer, cooking the pork and vegetables over the noodles for an easy and nutritious, low-fat supper.

ORIENTAL PORK AND VEGETABLES

Serves 4

1lb (450 g) pork tenderloin,
   trimmed and sliced
1 medium carrot, cut into julienne strips
¼ cup (45 mL) snow peas
1 medium red bell pepper, thinly sliced
2 celery ribs, cut into julienne strips
1 medium leek, halved and thinly sliced
2 garlic cloves, peeled and crushed Juice
   and zest of 1 medium orange
3 Tbsp (45 mL) dry sherry, such as fino
2 Tbsp (25 mL) light soy sauce
½ in (2.5 cm) piece fresh ginger, grated
4 cups (1 L) vegetable stock
1¼ cups (300 mL) dry egg noodles

❶ Place the pork and vegetables in a shallow glass dish. Mix the remaining ingredients (except the stock and noodles) together and pour over the ingredients in the dish. Cover and leave to marinate for at least 1 hour, turning occasionally.

❷ Transfer the ingredients, including the marinade, to a heatproof dish which fits the top of the steamer.

❸ Put the stock in the base of the steamer. Cover with a tight-fitting lid and steam over the stock for 20 minutes.

❹ Add the noodles to the stock, replace the upper tier, and continue steaming for a further 5 minutes until the pork and noodles are cooked. Watch not to overcook the noodles.

❺ Drain the noodles and place in a warm serving bowl. Top with the pork and vegetables, and serve immediately.

Dim sum are so easy to make and are great as an impressive party food or as a snack or appetizer. The thin dough is very simple to make, ensuring minimum effort for maximum impact.

PORK DIM SUM

Serves 4

For the dough

1 cup (250 mL) all-purpose flour

1 egg

2 tsp (10 mL) cold water

For the filling

6 oz (175 g) ground pork

1/3 cup (75 mL) button mushrooms, cleaned and finely chopped

3 scallions, chopped

1/2 small carrot, finely chopped

1 celery rib, finely chopped

2 Tbsp (25 mL) light soy sauce

1 tsp (5 mL) light sesame oil

1 tsp (5 mL) Chinese five-spice powder

For the dip

2 Tbsp (25 mL) dark soy sauce

1 medium green chile pepper, chopped

1/2 tsp (3 mL) dark sesame oil

2 tsp (10 mL) brown sugar

1 Tbsp (15 mL) sherry

1 Sift the flour into a mixing bowl and stir in the egg and water to make a firm dough. On a floured surface, roll into a sausage shape and cut into 28 slices.

2 Roll each slice into a 3-inch (7.5 cm) round.

3 Mix the filling ingredients together in a bowl and spoon into the center of each dough circle. Dampen the edge of each circle with water and fold up the sides to encase the filling, pinching the top together.

4 Put the dim sum in a stacking steamer lined with a clean damp tea towel, cover with the lid, and steam for 25 minutes until cooked through.

5 Meanwhile, mix the dip ingredients together and place in a serving bowl. Serve the dim sum, garnished with scallions and chile pepper.

If you don't like blue cheese, add any soft but strongly flavored cheese in its place for an equally delicious result. Cottage cheese may be sieved and used instead of ricotta cheese for a healthier alternative.

BLUE CHEESE EGG POTS WITH GARLIC SAUSAGE

Serves 4

6 Tbsp (75 mL) soft blue cheese
4 Tbsp (50 mL) milk
2 Tbsp (25 mL) fresh parsley, chopped
Salt and freshly ground black pepper
1 cup (250 mL) ricotta cheese
1 medium tomato, seeded and chopped
4 oz (100 g) garlic sausage, chopped
4 eggs

❶ Crumble the blue cheese into a mixing bowl and stir in the milk, parsley, and salt and pepper.

❷ Gradually blend in the ricotta cheese and stir in the tomato and sausage. Spoon the mixture into four ramekins and break an egg into each dish.

❸ Place the dishes in the steamer tiers, cover with a tight-fitting lid and steam for 6 to 8 minutes or until the egg is cooked, as desired. Serve immediately with toasted bread, or salad.

A filling and delicious lunch or supper dish, this variation on a fried rösti is also healthier, as there is no additional fat used. Vary the cheeses used according to personal taste, but be sure to use strongly flavored varieties.

CHEESE AND HAM ROSTI

Serves 4

3 cups (700 mL) potatoes, peeled
4 oz (100 g) smoked ham, cut into thin strips
½ cup (100 mL) freshly grated
   Cheddar cheese
¼ cup (50 mL) blue cheese, crumbled
3 Tbsp (45 mL) shelled walnuts, chopped
⅔ cup (120 mL) heavy cream or yogurt
3 eggs, beaten
2 Tbsp (25 mL) fresh parsley, chopped
Salt and freshly ground black pepper

❶ Grate the potatoes into a sieve and press well to remove excess water. Transfer to a mixing bowl. Add all of the remaining ingredients and mix well. Press into the base of a shallow, heatproof dish which fits into the steamer top.

❷ Cover with foil and place in the steamer, place a tight-fitting lid on top, and cook for 45 minutes or until the potatoes are cooked through. Serve immediately with a crisp salad.

This is such a simple dish, perfect for children or for a quick supper or light lunch. Other cooked meats, such as salami, may be used in place of the ham.

SMOKED HAM AND EGGS EN COCOTTE

Serves 4

1 cup (250 mL) fresh spinach

Butter, for greasing

4 oz (100 g) cooked smoked ham, cubed

4 eggs

Pinch of cayenne pepper

4 Tbsp (50 mL) light cream

❶ Blanch the spinach in a small amount of boiling water until just cooked, and drain well, squeezing out any excess moisture.

❷ Lightly grease four ramekins and place the spinach in the base of each.

❸ Top with the ham and then break an egg into each dish. Sprinkle with cayenne pepper and spoon the cream on top.

❹ Transfer the ramekins to the steamer tiers, cover with a tight-fitting lid and steam for 6 to 8 minutes or until the eggs are cooked, as desired. Serve with hot toast.

Steaming ribs gives a wonderfully tender result and a terrific flavor, accentuated here by a spicy sauce. Rubbing the ribs with salt before you start removes any excess moisture and juices which would otherwise come out during steaming and dilute the sauce. Be sure to rinse the ribs well and pat dry to remove the salt.

SPICY SPARERIBS

Serves 4

3 lb (1½ kg) pork spareribs

1 Tbsp (15 mL) salt

¾ cup (150 mL) chicken or pork stock

2 Tbsp (25 mL) dark soy sauce

1 tsp (5 mL) ground ginger

2 tsp (10 mL) dark sesame oil

2 Tbsp (25 mL) garlic, peeled and finely
 chopped

2 medium red chiles, very finely chopped

2 tsp (10 mL) dark brown sugar

4 Tbsp (50 mL) liquid honey

1 Tbsp (15 mL) tomato paste

2 Tbsp (25 mL) dry sherry

1½ cups (350 mL) long-grain white rice

2 Tbsp (25 mL) fresh cilantro, chopped

❶ Rinse ribs under cold water and pat dry. Rub the ribs with the salt and leave for 30 minutes. Rinse thoroughly and pat dry. Fill the steamer base with water and bring to a boil. Add the ribs and cook for 10 minutes. Drain, discarding the water in the steamer.

❷ Transfer the ribs to a heatproof bowl which fits the steamer top. Mix the stock, soy sauce, ginger, sesame oil, garlic, chiles, sugar, honey, tomato paste and sherry, and pour over the ribs.

❸ Place the ribs over the prepared steamer base, cover with a tight-fitting lid and cook for 1 hour or until cooked through.

❹ Meanwhile, halfway through the rib cooking time, add the rice to the steamer base water and cook for 15 minutes. Reduce the heat slightly and cook for a further 15 minutes until tender and fluffy. Remove the rice from the water before this if you prefer rice with a "bite." Stir in the cilantro and spoon onto a warmed serving plate. Top with the ribs and keep warm. Place the marinade juices in a small saucepan and bring to a boil. Boil rapidly to reduce by half and pour over the ribs. Serve immediately.

A Cajun Creole pilaf which was created in the eighteenth century, Jambalaya is thought to have derived its name from the Spanish word for ham – jamon, an essential ingredient of early recipes. Today, smoked sausage is used for flavor and chile provides the spice element. An economical dish, this version is lower in fat than most recipes, and steaming makes it quicker to cook, with the added advantage of a sealed pan retaining all of the exquisite flavors within the dish.

JAMBALAYA

Serves 4

¼ cup (50 mL) butter

1 large yellow bell pepper, roughly chopped

1 large red bell pepper, roughly chopped

1 large red onion, quartered and thinly sliced

2 celery ribs, thinly sliced

3 garlic cloves, peeled and crushed

1 large red chile pepper, finely chopped

3 large tomatoes, seeded and finely chopped

1 Tbsp (15 mL) tomato paste

Few drops of Tabasco Sauce

½ cup (100 mL) mixed long-grain white and wild rice

Salt and freshly ground black pepper

4 cups (1 L) vegetable stock

1 lb (450 g) large peeled, cooked shrimp

12 oz (350 g) smoked sausage, medium diced

⅓ cup (75 mL) peas

❶ Melt the butter in the base of the steamer pan and sauté the peppers, onion, celery, garlic, and chile pepper for 3 minutes, stirring.

❷ Add the tomatoes, tomato paste, Tabasco Sauce and rice, and season to taste. Stir in the stock and cover with a tight-fitting lid.

❸ Cook gently for 15 to 20 minutes. Add the shrimp, sausage, and peas, replace the lid, and continue cooking for a further 5 to 7 minutes until the rice is cooked through. Serve.

Steaming this classic recipe renders a flavorful and moist dish. Use ground beef as an alternative to the traditional lamb. Serve with a fresh, crisp salad and warm crusty bread.

MOUSSAKA

Serves 4

1 large eggplant

Salt

3 Tbsp (45 mL) olive oil

1 medium onion, halved and thinly sliced

2 garlic cloves, peeled and crushed

1 lb (450 g) cooked lamb, finely chopped

15 oz (426 mL) can chopped tomatoes

2 tsp (10 mL) dried mixed herbs

1 Tbsp (15 mL) Worcestershire sauce

2 Tbsp (25 mL) butter

2 Tbsp (25 mL) all-purpose flour

1¼ cup (300 mL) milk

1 egg, separated

¼ cup (50 mL) freshly grated Cheddar cheese

2 Tbsp (25 mL) freshly grated Parmesan cheese

❶ Slice the eggplant thin and place in a colander. Sprinkle with salt and leave for 30 minutes. Rinse under cold water and pat dry.

❷ Heat the oil in a skillet and cook the eggplant for 2 to 3 minutes. Remove from the pan and set aside. Add the onion and garlic to the skillet and cook over medium heat for 2 to 3 minutes, until softened.

❸ Remove the onion and garlic from the heat. Stir the lamb, tomatoes and herbs and Worcestershire sauce into the skillet and mix well.

❹ Arrange a layer of eggplant slices in the base of a deep heatproof serving dish. Top with meat mixture and the remaining eggplant.

❺ Melt butter in a saucepan. Whisk in flour. Stirring constantly, cook for 1 minute. Gradually add milk. Bring to a boil, stirring.

❻ Remove the pan from the heat and stir in the egg yolk and cheese. Whisk the egg white in a clean bowl until peaking and gently fold into the sauce. Pour over the meat mixture and cover with pleated foil, secured with string to prevent steam escaping and to secure a tight fit.

❼ Place the dish in the top of the steamer, cover tightly with the lid, and steam for 20 minutes. Serve sprinkled with the cheese, and a salad.

The cucumber and yogurt sauce lends a Greek tone to this tender lamb —a very refreshing fusion of flavors. The vegetables make for a very colorful dish.

LAMB WITH CHILLED YOGURT SAUCE

Serves 4

2 lb (900 g) lean lamb, cubed

3 garlic cloves, peeled and crushed

3 Tbsp (45 mL) olive oil

Juice and zest of 1 medium lemon

1 Tbsp (15 mL) fresh oregano, chopped

¼ cup (85 mL) red wine

Salt and freshly ground black pepper

1 medium yellow bell pepper, cubed

2 Tbsp (25 mL) pitted black olives, quartered

1 medium zucchini, cut into julienne strips

1 medium red onion, cut into eight

2 large tomatoes, seeded and chopped

6 Tbsp (85 mL) lamb stock

For the sauce

6 Tbsp (75 mL) cucumber, diced

2 garlic cloves, peeled and crushed

1 Tbsp (15 mL) fresh chives, chopped

1¼ cups (300 mL) Greek-style yogurt

❶ Put the lamb in a shallow glass dish. Mix together the garlic, 1½ tablespoons (20 mL) of oil, lemon juice and zest, oregano, wine and salt and pepper. Pour over the lamb, cover, and marinate for 2 hours, turning occasionally.

❷ Remove the lamb from the marinade with a slotted spoon, reserving the marinade. Heat the remaining oil in a skillet and brown the lamb, turning for 2 to 3 minutes. Add the bell pepper, olives, zucchini, onion and tomatoes, and cook for 2 to 3 minutes. Spoon the contents of the pan into a heatproof dish.

❸ Pour the stock into a saucepan along with the reserved marinade. Bring to a boil and cook until reduced to a thickened sauce (about 4 to 5 minutes). Pour over the lamb. Cover the dish tightly with pleated foil secured with string and place in the steamer top. Cover with a tight-fitting lid and steam for 30 to 35 minutes until the meat is cooked through.

❹ Meanwhile, mix the sauce ingredients together and chill until required. Serve with the lamb and freshly steamed rice.

If you don't have Madeira, use a dry sherry such as fino: the result will be equally delicious, although it is worth treating yourself to the real thing.

LAMB WITH MADEIRA SAUCE

Serves 4

4 lamb tenderloins (about 4 oz/100 g each)
4 Tbsp (50 mL) dry Madeira, such as Sercial
2 Tbsp (25 mL) lamb stock
1 tsp (5 mL) Worcestershire sauce
1 Tbsp (15 mL) fresh thyme, chopped
1 Tbsp (15 mL) tomato paste
⅓ cup (75 mL) mushrooms, washed
    and thinly sliced
1 medium orange bell pepper, thinly sliced
8 pearl onions
¼ cup (50 mL) green beans, halved
2 Tbsp (25 mL) butter

❶ Place the lamb in a shallow glass dish with the Madeira, stock, Worcestershire sauce, thyme, and tomato paste. Cover and leave to marinate for at least 1 hour.

❷ Remove the lamb from the dish, reserving the marinade, and place in a waxed paper-lined steamer tier with the vegetables. Cover with a tight-fitting lid and steam for 20 minutes or until cooked through.

❸ Meanwhile, heat the marinade in a small saucepan and whisk in the butter to make a glossy sauce. Serve with the lamb and vegetables and a bowl of freshly steamed rice.

This spicy peppercorn-encrusted lamb is ideal with a vegetable dish and mashed potatoes. For a milder dish, halve the quantity of peppercorns used.

LAMB WITH BACON PEPPERCORN SAUCE ON A BED OF CABBAGE

Serves 4

¼ cup (50 mL) mixed peppercorns
3 tsp (15 mL) prepared Dijon mustard
1½ lb (650 g) boneless shoulder of lamb,
    cubed
½ cup (100 mL) green cabbage, shredded
¾ cup (150 mL) lamb or chicken stock
¾ cup (150 mL) red wine
4 slices smoked bacon, diced
    (about 4 oz/100 g)
1 tsp (5 mL) light brown sugar
2 Tbsp (25 mL) butter
Salt and freshly ground black pepper

❶ Crush the peppercorns with a mortar and pestle or in a plastic bag using a rolling pin. Spread 2 teaspoons (10 mL) of the mustard over the lamb and coat in all but 1 tablespoon (15 mL) of the peppercorns.

❷ Arrange the cabbage in the center of a large square of foil and place the lamb on top. Bring up the sides to make a parcel, sealing the top.

❸ Place the parcel in the steamer tier, cover with a tight-fitting lid, and steam for 20 minutes or until cooked through. Leave the parcel sealed.

❹ Mix the stock, remaining mustard and peppercorns, wine, bacon and brown sugar in a small saucepan. Cook gently for 5 to 7 minutes.

❺ Gradually whisk the butter into the wine mixture to make a glossy sauce. Serve the lamb on the bed of cabbage with the sauce drizzled over.

Lamb chops are ideal for steaming as they are small and take little time to cook. Reduce the cooking time if you prefer lamb rare. If possible, marinate the lamb for a longer period of time, up to 4 hours, for a stronger, richer, flavor.

LAMB CHOPS WITH SPICY PEACH RELISH

Serves 4

8 lamb chops (about 3 oz/75 g each
   in weight)
2 Tbsp (25 mL) olive oil
2 garlic cloves, peeled and crushed
1 Tbsp (15 mL) lemon juice
1 Tbsp (15 mL) balsamic vinegar
2 Tbsp (25 mL) liquid honey
2 sprigs fresh rosemary

For the sauce
2 Tbsp (25 mL) butter
3 peaches, skinned, pitted and chopped
4 scallions, chopped
¾ cup (150 mL) lamb or vegetable stock
¾ cup (150 mL) peach juice
1 Tbsp (15 mL) sultana raisins
½ tsp (3 mL) ground cinnamon
1 tsp (5 mL) ground ginger
1 Tbsp (15 mL) cornstarch

❶ Put the lamb chops in a shallow glass dish. Mix the oil, garlic, lemon juice, vinegar, honey and rosemary, and pour over the lamb. Cover and marinate for at least 1 hour, turning occasionally.

❷ Meanwhile (for the sauce) melt the butter in a pan and add the remaining ingredients except the cornstarch. Transfer to a shallow heatproof dish which fits the steamer.

❸ Remove the lamb from the marinade and add to the sauce in the dish. Cover with plastic wrap and steam for 20 minutes or until the lamb is cooked through. Remove the lamb from the steamer and keep warm. Pour the sauce into a small saucepan. Blend the cornstarch to a paste with 2 tablespoons (25 mL) cold water and stir into the sauce. Bring to a boil, stirring until thickened and clear. Spoon over the lamb and serve with new potatoes and green vegetables.

The lamb takes on the rich, warm qualities of the port and rosemary for a full-flavored dish. Madeira or sherry could work equally as well as port, and any complementary preserve could be used.

LAMB FILLET WITH PORT AND GARLIC SAUCE

Serves 4

1 lb (450 g) boneless shoulder of lamb, cubed
2 sprigs fresh rosemary
1 garlic clove, peeled and crushed
2 Tbsp (25 mL) olive oil

For the sauce
¾ cup (150 mL) port
¼ cup (50 mL) lamb stock
2 garlic cloves, peeled and thinly sliced
1 tsp (5 mL) sugar
2 Tbsp (25 mL) red currant jelly
2 tsp (10 mL) cornstarch
Rosemary sprigs, to garnish

❶ Place the lamb in a shallow glass dish. Mix the rosemary, garlic and oil together, pour over the lamb and mix well. Cover and leave to marinate for 1 hour, turning occasionally.

❷ Meanwhile, pour the port and stock into a small saucepan and add the garlic, sugar and red currant jelly. Heat slowly until the jelly dissolves.

❸ Blend the cornstarch with 4 teaspoons (20 mL) of cold water and stir into the sauce. Bring to a boil until thickened and clear.

❹ Remove the lamb and rosemary from the marinade and spoon into a heatproof dish which fits the top of the steamer. Pour the sauce over the lamb and cover with a tight-fitting lid.

❺ Steam the lamb for 15 to 20 minutes until cooked through. Serve with fresh steamed vegetables and garnish with rosemary sprigs.

Beef and horseradish are a classic combination of flavors, and this dish is no exception. The sauce may be made in advance and reheated for serving. Creamed horseradish may be made by mixing 4 Tbsp (60 mL) prepared horseradish sauce and 1 Tbsp (15 mL) sour cream together, or bought ready-made.

MEATBALLS WITH HORSERADISH SAUCE

Serves 4

1 lb (450 g) ground beef

1 egg

1 celery rib, finely chopped

1 Tbsp (15 mL) tomato paste

1 Tbsp (15 mL) fresh basil, chopped

1 Tbsp (15 mL) pitted green olives,
  finely chopped

1 shallot, finely chopped

1 tsp (5 mL) Worcestershire sauce

Salt and freshly ground black pepper

4 Tbsp (50mL) fine bread crumbs

For the sauce

2 Tbsp (25 mL) butter

2 Tbsp (25 mL) all-purpose flour

$\frac{1}{4}$ cups (300 mL) milk

$1\frac{3}{4}$ cup (150 mL) dry white wine

1 large bunch basil, leaves only,
  washed and shredded

2 Tbsp (25 mL) prepared creamed
  horseradish sauce

To serve

$\frac{1}{2}$ cup (100 mL) brown rice

$2\frac{1}{2}$ cups (600 mL) vegetable stock

① Put the ingredients for the meatballs in a food processor or blender and blend for 30 seconds until combined, or mix well by hand. Roll into walnut-sized balls.

② Put the rice and stock in the base of the steamer and bring to a boil. Arrange the meatballs on a sheet of dampened wax paper in the top of the steamer and cover with a tight-fitting lid. Cook with the rice for 20 minutes until the rice and meatballs are cooked through. Check the rice after 15 minutes to make sure it doesn't overcook.

③ Meanwhile, melt the butter for the sauce in a pan and whisk in the flour. Cook, stirring, for 1 minute. Gradually stir in the milk and wine, and bring to a boil, stirring constantly.

④ Add the remaining sauce ingredients and cook for 5 minutes. Blend in a food processor for 30 seconds until smooth.

⑤ Drain the rice and spoon onto a warmed serving plate. Arrange the meatballs on top and spoon on the sauce. Serve immediately.

If a less than prime cut of beef is used, tenderize the meat with a mallet before cooking. The basil gives an aromatic flavor to the dish, but if unavailable, oregano may be used.

PEPPERED BEEF TENDERLOIN WITH BASIL TOMATO SAUCE

Serves 4

1 lb (450 g) top round steak
2 Tbsp (25 mL) peppercorns

For the sauce
4 Tbsp (50 mL) dry sherry
1 cup (200 mL) puréed tomatoes
2 scallions, sliced
2 Tbsp (25 mL) fresh basil, shredded
1 tsp (5 mL) light brown sugar

① Tenderize the meat with a mallet and cut into four equal-size pieces.

② Crush the peppercorns in a mortar and pestle or in a plastic bag with a rolling pin and press into the beef on both sides.

③ Transfer the beef to a steamer tier, cover with a tight-fitting lid, and steam for 15 minutes or until cooked through.

④ Meanwhile, place all of the sauce ingredients in a small saucepan and bring to a boil. Reduce the heat and simmer for 10 minutes.

⑤ Remove the beef from the steamer and serve with the sauce and fresh steamed vegetables, and boiled potatoes.

Although this recipe is a little time-consuming, it is well worth the effort. Feel free to use other meats and vegetables that you have on hand for variation of fillings. It is important to cover the dough with a damp cloth to allow it to rest without drying out.

SPICY BEEF RAVIOLI

Serves 4

For the ravioli dough

1 cup (200 mL) all-purpose flour

¼ cup (50 mL) rice semolina

Pinch of salt

4 tsp (20 mL) olive oil

2 eggs, beaten

3–4 Tbsp (45–50 mL) milk

For the filling

4 oz (100 g) ground beef

1 small onion, finely chopped

1 small carrot, finely diced

½ tsp (3 mL) ground cumin

½ tsp (3 mL) ground coriander

Pinch of paprika

2 tsp (10 mL) fresh thyme, chopped

1 Tbsp (15 mL) tomato paste

Salt and freshly ground black pepper

For the sauce

6 Tbsp (75 mL) butter

3 tsp (15 mL) lemon juice

3 Tbsp (45 mL) vegetable stock

2 Tbsp (25 mL) red wine

Pinch of dry mustard

1 garlic clove, peeled and crushed

3 Tbsp (45 mL) fresh mixed herbs, chopped

Parmesan strips, to garnish

❶ Make the pasta dough by sifting the flour into a mixing bowl. Add the semolina and salt and make a well in the center.

❷ Place the oil, beaten eggs, and 1 tablespoon (15 mL) of milk in the well and gradually mix into the flour and rice semolina to make a firm dough, adding more milk if necessary to give a smooth dough. On a lightly floured board, knead the dough and cover with a damp cloth for 30 minutes.

❸ Mix the filling ingredients together and put on a heatproof plate. Place in the top of a warm steamer, cover with a tight-fitting lid and steam for 20 minutes until cooked through. Allow to cool.

4 Cut the pasta dough into 8 equal pieces. Dust a work surface with flour and roll one piece of the pasta dough to an 8 inch (20 cm) x 4 inch (10 cm) rectangle; the dough should be quite thin, but still hold together. Repeat with the other seven pieces of dough. Brush four pieces of dough with water and spoon small quantities of the filling at regular intervals on the dough.

5 Place the other four sheets of dough on top, pressing down between the piles of filling to make sealed squares. Cut out each square with a knife or fluted cutter. Leave to dry on a clean dish towel for 2 hours.

6 Fill the steamer base with water and bring to a boil. Cook the ravioli in the water for 5 minutes. Remove with a slotted spoon and transfer to a heatproof bowl, small enough to fit into the steamer.

7 Mix the sauce ingredients together and add to the bowl. Place in the steamer top and cover with a tight-fitting lid. Steam for 5 to 7 minutes until cooked through. Serve immediately.

Fresh calf's liver is ideal for steaming. It will remain moist and tender and served in a mustard wine sauce, is a real treat. Try it, especially if you think you've never liked liver. Full of iron, it's a highly nutritious meat.

LIVER IN A HERBED MUSTARD SAUCE

Serves 4

1 lb (450 g) calf's liver
¾ cup (150 mL) red wine
1 garlic clove, peeled and crushed
2 tsp (10 mL) fresh sage, chopped
1 medium leek, finely sliced
1 large carrot, cut into julienne strips

For the sauce
1 Tbsp (15 mL) butter
1 Tbsp (15 mL) all-purpose flour
5 Tbsp (65 mL) plain yogurt or light cream
2 Tbsp (25 mL) fresh sage, chopped
Salt and freshly ground black pepper

1 Cut the liver into thin strips and place in a shallow glass dish. Mix the wine, garlic, and sage, and pour over the liver. Cover and marinate for 1 hour, turning occasionally.

2 Remove the liver, reserving the marinade, and place in a wax paper-lined steamer tier with the vegetables. Cover with a tight-fitting lid and steam for 10 minutes or until cooked through.

3 Meanwhile, melt the butter for the sauce in a small pan and stir in the flour. Remove from the heat and add the marinade, yogurt or cream and sage. Return to the heat and heat gently without boiling, stirring until thickened. Season to taste.

4 Place the liver and vegetables on a warmed plate, and top with the sauce. Garnish with sage and serve with boiled potatoes.

If you're looking for a plain steamed pudding, you've come to the wrong book! The following desserts are a mile away from the traditional, stodgy steamed desserts of yesteryear.

Many of the delicious fruits now available are perfect for steaming, whether on a skewer, in a brulée, marinated, or served with a luxurious sauce. These desserts are light and refreshing, packed with color, flavor and natural goodness — although there are a couple of "naughty but nice" recipes for those of us who really can't resist.

DESSERTS

Adding sweet potato to bananas gives great color, texture and flavor to this warm dessert, perfect for a cold winter evening.

STEAMED BANANAS IN ORANGE SAUCE

Serves 4

¾ cup (170 mL) sweet potato, peeled and cubed

4 large ripe bananas

2 Tbsp (25 mL) light brown sugar

8 Tbsp (100 mL) orange juice

Zest of 1 medium orange

2 Tbsp (25 mL) orange liqueur

Fresh mint or lemon balm leaves, to decorate

Heavy cream or vanilla yogurt, to serve

1 Boil the sweet potato in water in the base of the steamer for 10 minutes. Remove with a slotted spoon.

2 Cut four large sheets of foil and place one-quarter of the sweet potato in the center of each.

3 Cut the bananas in half lengthwise and place one banana on top of each parcel. Sprinkle with sugar and fold up the sides of the foil but don't seal.

4 Spoon the orange juice and zest, and the liqueur into the parcels and fold the top of the foil over to seal.

5 Steam the fruit in the top of the steamer, covered, for 5 minutes until hot and the sugar has melted. Decorate with fresh mint, and serve with heavy cream or vanilla yogurt.

This is a seasonal dish, capturing the wonderful warm flavors and aromas of winter. It may be made with segmented sweet oranges when clementines are unavailable.

FRESH FIGS WITH CLEMENTINES

Serves 4

8 small clementines, peeled,
   with pith removed
6 Tbsp (75 mL) orange juice
2 Tbsp (25 mL) brandy
1 Tbsp (15 mL) Grenadine syrup (optional)
1 Tbsp (15 mL) light brown sugar
16 medium fresh figs
Plain yogurt, to serve
Fresh mint sprigs and pared orange or
   lemon zest, to decorate

1 Place the clementines in a heatproof dish and place in a steamer tier.

2 Pour the orange juice, brandy and Grenadine, if using, into a small saucepan, add the sugar, and heat gently to dissolve. Bring to a boil.

3 Add the figs to the clementines, pour the syrup over, and cover with a tight-fitting lid. Steam for 15 minutes.

4 Spoon the fruit into a serving dish, with a little of the syrup around. Decorate and serve.

This combination of fruit makes a real splash of color and flavor on the plate. If you prefer crêpes – and are skilled at making them – they work equally well.

FRUIT PUREE WITH WAFFLES AND CREAM

Serves 4

2 kiwi fruit
1 papaya
1 small pineapple

To serve
¾ cup (150 mL) plain yogurt
1 medium passionfruit
4 prepared waffles
Fresh mint sprigs, to decorate

❶ Halve the kiwi fruit and scoop the flesh onto the center of a foil square. Bring up the sides of the foil to make a sealed parcel.

❷ Peel, halve, seed and chop the papaya, place the flesh in another foil square, and seal well.

❸ Peel, core and chop the pineapple, place the flesh into another foil parcel, and place all three parcels in the top of the steamer. Cover with the lid, and steam for 10 minutes until hot.

❹ Either press each fruit separately through a strainer or blend in a food processor, until smooth. Cut the passion fruit in half and scoop out the seeds and flesh. Mix with the yogurt and serve with the three fruit syrups, spooned over the waffles. Decorate with mint, and serve.

Brulée is an all-time favorite dessert with most people, and very simple to prepare and cook in a steamer. Canned plums will work, though of course fresh is always preferred. Other stored fruits such as cherries, peaches or nectarines may also be used as alternatives.

PLUM BRULEE

Serves 4

4 medium ripe plums, pitted and chopped
2 Tbsp (25 mL) Kirsch
2 cups (450 mL) heavy cream
1 tsp (5 mL) vanilla extract
4 egg yolks
2 Tbsp (25 mL) almonds, chopped
3 Tbsp (45 mL) demerara or brown sugar

❶ Place the plums in the base of four lightly buttered ramekins and spoon a quarter of the Kirsch over each.

❷ Heat the cream in a saucepan until just below boiling point but do not boil. Remove from the heat and stir in the vanilla extract, egg yolks and nuts.

❸ Pour the cream over the plums and place in the top of the steamer. Cover and steam for 10 minutes. Remove from the steamer and chill for 4 hours.

❹ Sprinkle the tops of the brulées with sugar and cook under a hot broiler for 3 to 4 minutes until the sugar caramelizes, but do not let it blacken and burn. Return the brulée to the refrigerator until the topping hardens, and serve, decorated with fresh plums.

This is a little like a berry pie with a nutty batter top. Choose a good variety of fresh, seasonal berries for flavor. A dollop of vanilla extract in the cream or yogurt is a nice touch.

BERRY CLAFOUTI

Serves 4

2¾ cups (650 mL) mixed berries, such as blackberries, raspberries and strawberries, washed

2 Tbsp (25 mL) light brown sugar

4 Tbsp (50 mL) toasted slivered almonds

For the batter

¾ cup (175 mL) all-purpose flour

2 Tbsp (25 mL) ground almonds

1 tsp (5 mL) baking powder

2 Tbsp (25 mL) light brown sugar

¾ cup (150 mL) milk

1 egg, separated

Yogurt or cream, to serve

❶ Put the fruit in the base of a heatproof, shallow dish which fits the top of the steamer, and sprinkle the sugar on top.

❷ Mix all of the batter ingredients together except the egg white. Whisk the egg white until peaking and gently fold into the batter. Spoon over the fruit in the bowl and scatter the almonds on top.

❸ Cover the dish with pleated foil and secure with string. Cook, covered, in the steamer for 1 to 1¼ hours or until the batter is cooked through.

❹ Remove the foil and serve immediately with yogurt or cream.

Once filled, this cake should be stored in the refrigerator and eaten within a day, which won't be a problem. If using fresh banana slices to decorate the cake top, be sure to first mix them up with a bit of lemon juice, to prevent discoloration.

PECAN-BANANA CAKE

Serves 4

½ cup (100 mL) butter

½ cup (100 mL) light brown sugar

2 eggs, beaten

3 medium bananas, mashed

4 Tbsp (50 mL) self-rising whole wheat flour

4 Tbsp (50 mL) all-purpose flour

½ cup (100 mL) pecans, chopped

4 Tbsp (50 mL) sultana raisins

1 Tbsp (15 mL) lemon juice

4 Tbsp (50 mL) plain yogurt

For the filling

1 large ripe banana, mashed

2 Tbsp (25 mL) icing sugar, sifted

Juice of ½ medium lemon

¾ cup (150 mL) cream cheese

2 Tbsp (25 mL) plain yogurt

Chopped pecans and dried or fresh banana
   slices, to decorate

❶ Lightly grease the bases of two 7-inch (17.5 cm) sponge cake tins. Line with wax paper.

❷ Cream the butter and light brown sugar until light, and gradually beat in the eggs. Stir in the mashed bananas and fold in the flours, nuts, sultanas, lemon juice and yogurt. Spoon into the prepared tins and cover with pleated wax paper, secured with string.

❸ Place a cake tin in each tier of the steamer, cover and steam for 1¼ hours, changing the tiers over halfway through cooking time, or until cooked through.

❹ Allow the cakes to cool slightly before turning out to cool completely on a wire rack.

❺ Mix the banana, icing sugar, yogurt, lemon juice and cream cheese together for the filling, and spread over the top of the each cake. Stack the two layers and decorate the top with chopped pecan nuts and dried bananas, slice and serve.

Chocolate sponge pudding must be top of the list with most people, especially when served hot with whipped cream flavored with rum.

HOT CHOCOLATE PUDDING

Serves 4

½ cup (100 mL) dark chocolate, grated

2 Tbsp (25 mL) milk

2 Tbsp (25 mL) brandy

1 cup (250 mL) all-purpose flour

½ cup (100 mL) butter or
  margarine, softened

4 Tbsp (50 mL) dark brown sugar

2 Tbsp (25 mL) ground almonds

2 eggs, beaten

1 Tbsp (15 mL) coffee extract or very
  strong coffee, cooled

Icing sugar and grated semi-sweet
  chocolate, for decoration

❶ Lightly butter a 1-quart (1 L) pudding dish. Slowly melt the chocolate with the milk and brandy in a bowl over hot water.

❷ Sift the flour into a mixing bowl and cut in the butter until the mixture resembles bread crumbs. Stir in the sugar, ground almonds, eggs, coffee extract and melted chocolate mixture.

❸ Spoon the batter into the pudding dish, cover with pleated wax paper and foil secured with string. Steam, covered, for 1½ to 2 hours or until a knife inserted in the center comes out clean.

❹ Turn the pudding out onto a warmed serving plate, dust with icing sugar, and sprinkle with grated chocolate. Serve hot with custard or cream on the side.

Dried fruits have an intense flavor, and take on other flavors such as orange and alcohol with wonderful results. Serving them as kebobs makes them even more tempting.

SPICED FRUIT KEBOBS

Serves 4

12 pitted prunes
12 dried apricots
8 pieces dried mango
8 dried apple rings
Juice of 1 medium orange
2 Tbsp (25 mL) orange liqueur or
    sweetened orange juice
1 tsp (5 mL) ground cinnamon
Pinch ground nutmeg
4 cloves

For the sauce
⅓ cup (75 mL) cream cheese
½ cup (100 mL) plain yogurt
1 Tbsp (15 mL) liquid honey

❶ Place all of the fruit in a shallow glass dish. Mix the juice of the orange, liqueur or sweetened orange juice, and spices, and pour over the fruits. Cover and leave to marinate for 1 hour, turning occasionally.

❷ Remove the fruit from the marinade, reserving the liquid, and thread onto four halved wooden skewers. Place in the steamer over boiling water, cover with a tight-fitting lid, and steam for 10 minutes.

❸ Meanwhile, mix the marinade with the cream cheese, yogurt, and honey.

❹ Remove the skewers from the steamer and serve with the sauce.

This dish is great served hot or cold with thin wafers, almond thins or tuiles. A rich red wine could be used in place of the port. Arrowroot, a thickening agent that doesn't yield a chalky taste, is preferable to cornstarch.

PEARS IN PORT

Serves 4

4 large ripe sweet pears
¾ cup (150 mL) ruby port
6 Tbsp (75 mL) light brown sugar
2 Tbsp (25 mL) cherry preserves
½ tsp (3 mL) ground cinnamon
Grated zest of 1 medium orange
2 tsp (10 mL) arrowroot or cornstarch
Orange segments, to decorate

❶ Peel the pears and remove the cores. Place in a deep dish which fits the steamer.

❷ Heat the port, sugar, preserves, cinnamon and orange zest in a pan until the preserves melt. Pour over the pears.

❸ Cover with pleated waxed paper, secure with string, and cover with the lid. Steam for 15 to 18 minutes until the pears are cooked through but not falling apart. Remove the pears from the syrup and place on serving plates.

❹ Transfer the port to a small saucepan and whisk in the arrowroot. Bring to a boil, stirring constantly until the sauce is thickened and clear. Spoon the sauce over the pears and decorate with orange segments. Serve warm.

This is a really attractive way to serve an old favorite. Adding mint to the rice gives it a subtle flavor which is particularly enjoyable with the fresh raspberry sauce.

RICE PUDDING CASTLES WITH RASPBERRY COULIS

Serves 4

¾ cup (150 mL) short grain rice

1 cup (250 mL) milk

¼ cup (50 mL) heavy cream

4 Tbsp (50 mL) demerara or brown sugar

Pinch of grated or ground nutmeg

2 Tbsp (25 mL) fresh mint, chopped

1 tsp (5 mL) vanilla extract

2 Tbsp (25 mL) chopped toasted hazelnuts

For the sauce

1 cup (250 mL) raspberries, fresh,
  or thawed if frozen

2 Tbsp (25 mL) icing sugar

1 tsp (5 mL) almond extract

1 Mix the rice, milk, cream, sugar, nutmeg, mint, vanilla and nuts, and spoon into four molds. Cover with pleated foil secured with string.

2 Place the molds in the steamer tiers, cover with the lid, and steam for 1 hour or until set.

3 Meanwhile, put the sauce ingredients in a food processor or blender, and purée until smooth. Press through a sieve to remove any seeds. Turn the puddings out onto serving plates and spoon the sauce over. Serve immediately.

Usually a lengthy dish to prepare, this Charlotte Russe is quick, simple and really delicious. Be sure to pack the ladyfingers tightly around the basin to keep the coffee custard in place. You can find ready-made ladyfingers at most supermarkets. Serve with ½ cup whipped heavy cream or thick yogurt flavored with 2 tsp brandy.

COFFEE CHARLOTTE RUSSE

Serves 4

2 large ripe pears, peeled,
  cored, and chopped

4 Tbsp (50 mL) brandy

¾ cup (170 mL) ladyfingers

2 cups (450 mL) whole milk

4 eggs

1 cup (200 mL) granulated light brown sugar

2 Tbsp (25 mL) coffee liqueur

Brandy-flavor cream or yogurt, to serve

1 Soak the pears in the brandy, turning frequently, for at least 20 minutes.

2 Line the sides of a greased 1-quart (1 L) straight-sided mold or casserole dish with ladyfingers and fill the base with the remaining fingers, chopped.

3 Add the pears and brandy to the center of the mold.

4 Heat the milk until almost boiling, but do not let boil. Remove from the heat.

5 Beat the eggs and sugar together, and stir in the coffee liqueur. Stir into the milk, and gently pour into the mold. Cover with plastic wrap and place in the steamer.

6 Cover with a tight-fitting lid and steam over simmering water for 40 to 50 minutes until set. Leave to cool completely before unmolding to serve. Serve with brandy-flavored cream or yogurt.

This is a great alternative way to serve fruit salad; served warm, the flavors meld together wonderfully. Use a variety of fruit on hand as preferred, making sure there is a good combination of colors and that the fruit is fairly firm in texture.

STEAMED TROPICAL FRUIT KEBOBS

Serves 4

1 large star fruit, thickly sliced
1 medium papaya
1 small cantaloupe melon
12 seedless green grapes
2 large slices fresh pineapple

For the marinade
2 Tbsp (25 mL) Kirsch
¾ cup (150 mL) orange juice
Juice of 1 medium lemon
2 Tbsp (25 mL) superfine sugar
2 tsp (10 mL) arrowroot or cornstarch

To serve
Small prepared sweet pancakes or crêpes
Heavy cream or plain yogurt

❶ Place the sliced star fruit and grapes in a shallow glass dish. Seed and chop the papaya, and add to the dish. With a melon baller, scoop the flesh from the melon and add to the dish. Cut the pineapple into chunks and add to the fruit.

❷ Mix all of the marinade ingredients and pour over the fruit. Cover with plastic wrap and chill for 2 hours, stirring occasionally.

❸ Remove the fruit from the marinade, reserving the liquid. Thread the fruit onto four halved wooden skewers, and set in the steamer top. Place the pancakes in the lower tier of the steamer, cover and cook for 10 minutes until hot.

❹ Meanwhile heat the marinade in a small pan. Whisk in the arrowroot and bring to a boil, stirring until thickened and clear. Arrange the pancakes on small serving plates, and top with cream. Serve the kebobs with the pancakes and syrup.

The slight tartness of the apricot sauce served with these stuffed, steamed apples complements well the apples' cinnamony sweetness. Other fruit, such as peaches or mango, would make an equally delicious sauce. Choose an apple suitable for baking.

STUFFED APPLES WITH APRICOT SAUCE

Serves 4

4 medium cooking apples
   (about 225 g/8 oz each)
2 tsp (10 mL) light brown sugar
1 Tbsp (15 mL) dried apricots, chopped
1 Tbsp (15 mL) sultana raisins
1 Tbsp (15 mL) dried dates,
   pitted and chopped
¼ tsp (2 mL) ground cinnamon
¼ tsp (2 mL) grated fresh or ground nutmeg
2 Tbsp (25 mL) butter, melted

For the sauce
6 fresh or canned apricots, peeled,
   pitted and chopped
Juice of 1 medium orange
½ tsp (3 mL) almond extract
1 Tbsp (15 mL) light brown sugar
Fresh mint sprigs, to decorate

❶ Core the apples. Mix the dried fruits, sugar and spices in a bowl, and stir in the butter to bind.

❷ Spoon the mixture into the cored apples and place in a steamer tier.

❸ Mix all of the sauce ingredients together in a heatproof bowl which fits the steamer and place in the second tier, over the apples.

❹ Place both tiers over boiling water, cover with a tight-fitting lid, and steam for 15 minutes until the apples are cooked through and the skins begin to split around the center.

❺ Keep the apples warm and pour the sauce into a food processor or blender. Blend for 30 seconds until smooth. Transfer the apples to a serving plate and spoon the sauce around. Decorate and serve immediately.

This is such a simple yet truly wonderful dessert. Served with almond biscuits, the apples are irresistible and sure to impress. While you could, in a pinch, use an inexpensive apple brandy, Calvados is well worth the cost (and great with fresh, sliced apples).

CALVADOS APPLES WITH MINT CREAM

Serves 4

4 Tbsp (50 mL) Calvados or apple brandy

Juice of 2 large oranges

1 Tbsp (15 mL) orange liqueur

2 Tbsp (25 mL) liquid honey

4 medium red dessert apples
  (about 5 oz/150 g each)

½ cinnamon stick, bruised

For the cream

¾ cup (150 mL) heavy cream, whipped

¾ cup (150 mL) plain yogurt

1 Tbsp (15 mL) liquid honey

2 Tbsp (25 mL) fresh mint, chopped

❶ Bring the Calvados, orange juice, liqueur and honey to a boil in a small saucepan.

❷ Meanwhile, cut the apples into quarters and remove the cores. Place in a heatproof bowl and pour the syrup over the top. Add the cinnamon stick and cover with pleated foil.

❸ Place the bowl in the steamer, cover with a tight-fitting lid, and steam for 15 minutes until the apples are tender, but not soft.

❹ Meanwhile, whip the cream and fold in the remaining ingredients together. Transfer to a serving dish and chill until required.

❺ Remove the apples from the Calvados syrup and arrange on serving plates. Spoon the sauce over the top, decorate with mint and serve with the cream on the side.

These individual puddings have a comforting warmth of flavors, beautifully set off by the tangy sauce. For a different dessert, add 2 Tbsp (25 mL) strong coffee and 2 Tbsp (25 mL) extra flour.

GINGER-ORANGE PUDDINGS

Serves 4

²/₃ cup (120 mL) butter or
    margarine, softened

½ cup (100 mL) light brown sugar

2 eggs, beaten

2 pieces preserved ginger, finely chopped

2 Tbsp (25 mL) corn syrup

½ tsp (3 mL) baking soda

2 Tbsp (25 mL) orange juice

Zest of 1 medium orange

Pinch of ground ginger

1 cup (250 mL) all-purpose flour

To serve

1¼ cups (300 mL) plain yogurt

Zest and juice of ½ small orange

2 tsp (10 mL) icing sugar, sifted

Orange zest and segments, to decorate

1 Grease the insides of four ramekins using 1 tablespoon (15 mL) of the butter. Beat the remaining butter and the sugar together until light and fluffy. Gradually beat in the eggs, ginger, syrup, baking soda, orange juice and zest, and ground ginger to taste.

2 Fold in the flour and spoon into the prepared ramekins. Cover with pleated foil and secure with string.

3 Place the dishes in the steamer, cover with a tight-fitting lid, and cook for 30 minutes or until a toothpick inserted into the puddings comes out clean.

4 Meanwhile, mix the sauce ingredients together, and chill. Turn the cooked puddings out onto a serving plate, decorate with orange zest and segments and serve with the sauce.

Crème caramel is a classic favorite. Usually cooked in the oven, it is perfect when steamed, and takes on a new twist with rich, sugar-glazed pineapple. Any firm fruit could be glazed and served in this way, such as mango, pears or peaches.

CREME CARAMEL WITH GLAZED PINEAPPLE

Serves 4

1 cup (200 mL) sugar
4 Tbsp (50 mL) cold water
1¾ cups (400 mL) whole milk
3 eggs

For the pineapple
2 Tbsp (25 mL) butter
1 Tbsp (15 mL) dark brown sugar
4 rings fresh pineapple, cubed
    (about 10 oz/300 g each)

❶ Place 4 tablespoons (50 mL) of the sugar in a heavy saucepan with the water, and heat until the sugar dissolves. Increase the heat until the sugar syrup turns dark brown, being careful not to burn. Remove from the heat and pour into four ramekins, turning to coat the base and sides.

❷ Heat the milk until almost boiling. Do not boil or the custard will not set properly and will cook. Beat the remaining sugar and eggs together, and gradually pour in the milk.

❸ Pour the custard into the ramekins and then wrap each dish in plastic wrap.

❹ Place in the steamer tier and cover with a tight-fitting lid. Cook over simmering water for 10 minutes, or until set. Leave to cool completely before unmolding to serve.

❺ Before serving, melt the butter in a skillet and add the sugar. Once the sugar has dissolved, stir in the pineapple pieces and cook for 4 to 5 minutes until glazed. Serve with the unmolded crème caramels.

Pears and chocolate are a classic combination. Be sure to choose ripe pears and four of roughly equal size. Orange liqueur or strong cooled coffee could be used as a flavoring instead of the dark rum.

PEARS WITH RUM AND CHOCOLATE SAUCE

Serves 4

4 medium sweet, ripe pears
Juice of ¹⁄₂ medium orange
   (reserve zest to decorate)
³⁄₄ cup (150 mL) dark chocolate
2 Tbsp (25 mL) dark rum
¹⁄₂ cup (100 mL) heavy cream
Grated dark and white chocolate, to decorate

❶ Peel the pears and brush them with the orange juice. Put the pears in the first steamer tier.

❷ Break the chocolate into a heatproof bowl which fits inside the steamer tier. Add the rum and cream, cover with pleated foil, and place over the pears. Cover with a tight-fitting lid.

❸ Cook the pears and sauce ingredients for 15 to 20 minutes or until the pears are cooked through, but not falling apart.

❹ Stir the chocolate sauce to combine the ingredients. Spoon the pears onto serving plates and top with the sauce. Decorate and serve.

This is one of those really quick desserts which is filled with both flavor and color. It can be prepared and cooked almost on the spur of the moment with fruit you have on hand such as apples, pears or bananas. Use the syrup from the stem ginger to flavor the fruit.

HOT MANGO AND KIWI IN GINGER SYRUP

Serves 4

2 large ripe mangoes, peeled,
   pitted and cubed
3 ripe kiwi fruit, peeled and cut into eight
2 pieces preserved stem ginger,
   each cut into eight
6 Tbsp (50 mL) ginger syrup
Juice of 1 medium lime
Lime zest, to decorate
Ginger snaps and yogurt, to serve

❶ Place the fruit in the center of a large square of foil. Bring up the sides, folding to form an open parcel.

❷ Mix the remaining ingredients together and pour over the fruit. Seal the parcel and place in the steamer.

❸ Cover with a tight-fitting lid and steam for 10 minutes. Remove from the steamer, decorate with lime zest, and serve with ginger snaps and plain or vanilla yogurt.

These individual puddings benefit from marinating in the alcohol and fruit juice. The fruit may be prepared up to 4 hours in advance and left to stand, for an easy dessert. Use a variety of fruit such as cherries, pears, apples, mangoes and pineapple for a really interesting dish.

MIXED FRUIT COBBLER WITH BRANDY SAUCE

Serves 4

For the fruit

1¼ cups (300 mL) mixed
   dried fruit, chopped
3 Tbsp (45 mL) brandy
4 Tbsp (50 mL) orange juice
1 tsp (5 mL) allspice

For the batter

2 eggs
2 Tbsp (25 mL) all-purpose flour
3 Tbsp (45 mL) sugar
1¼ cups (300 mL) milk

For the sauce

6 Tbsp (75 mL) granulated sugar
3 Tbsp (45 mL) boiling water
3 Tbsp (45 mL) brandy
2 Tbsp (25 mL) unsalted butter

1 Soak the fruit in the brandy, orange juice and allspice for 1 hour. Spoon into the base of four individual dishes.

2 Beat the eggs and whisk in the flour and then the sugar. Whisk in the milk to make a smooth batter.

3 Pour the batter over the fruit and wrap each dish in plastic wrap.

4 Place the dishes in the steamer, cover with a tight-fitting lid, and cook for 20 minutes or until the batter has set.

5 Meanwhile make the sauce. Dissolve the granulated sugar in a heavy pan and increase the heat until the sugar turns brown. Be careful not to burn. Remove from the heat and add the boiling water and the brandy. Return to the heat.

6 Gradually whisk in the butter, stirring constantly, until fully incorporated and glossy. Serve with the puddings.

*T*his chapter is designed to show how versatile and economical the steamer is. If you have an electric steamer with several stacking tiers and rice bowl, you will be able to create complete meals just using the one steamer, all timed to perfection.

Using recipes chosen from the previous chapters, the following are suggested menus for you to try, but feel free to experiment and substitute your own favorites, and you'll soon discover how simple and delicious "Steam Cuisine" really is.

MENUS

MENU 1

• Pork Dim Sum • Quick Salmon with Pesto • Steamed Bananas in Orange Sauce

1½ hrs	1 hr	35–40 mins	30 mins	10 mins
Make up the pesto sauce, cover and store in the refrigerator. Prepare the Dim Sum ready to cook and place in the steamer tier. Make up the dip.	Boil sweet potato for Steamed Bananas in Orange Sauce. Prepare the remaining ingredients except the bananas.	Finish Steamed Bananas in Orange Sauce, seal the parcels ready for cooking.	Cook the Dim Sum in the prepared steamer for 25 mins.	Fill steamer base, cook pasta with salmon over the top for 10 mins. Drain pasta and keep warm with salmon. Serve Dim Sum. Serve Salmon and pasta. Cook bananas for 5 mins and serve.

MENU 2

• Hot Lobster Salad • Caribbean Chicken • Plum Brulée

4½ hrs	1½ hrs	1 hr	20 mins	5 mins
Heat water in steamer base. Prepare brulée, steam for 10 mins. Remove and chill in the refrigerator for 4 hours.	Prepare chicken, sauté in base of steamer, add remaining ingredients, cover and cook for 1 hour. Boil the rice for chicken for 15 mins. Drain and set aside.	Prepare lobster and vegetables, place in steamer ready to cook. Mix dressing ingredients in a pan. Top brulée with sugar, grill 3–4 mins. Return to refrigerator.	Cook rice in steamer over chicken for 15 mins. Set lobster salad over rice, cook 15 mins. Place salad greens in bowl. Cook the pineapple for 5 mins.	Serve lobster salad appetizer. Keep chicken, rice and pineapple warm, serve as main course. Serve brulée as dessert.

MENU 3

• Zucchini and Beans with Garlic and Mint • Paella • Crème Caramel with Glazed Pineapple

2 hrs	1 hr	30–40 mins	5 mins
Prepare and cook the Crème Caramel. Chill in the refrigerator ready to serve. Prepare the pineapple for the dessert.	Prepare Paella ingredients, sauté the chicken, salami, garlic, pepper and rice 5 mins. Add stock, seasoning, cayenne and saffron.	Cover Paella, cook over gentle heat for 15 mins. Add remaining ingredients, cook appetizer over the top for 10 mins. Cook pineapple for dessert, keep warm. Unmold crème caramels, decorate and serve.	Remove Paella from heat, place in serving dish, keep warm. Serve Zucchini starter, followed by the Paella and then the Crème Caramel desserts.

MENU 4

• Spicy Beets with Orange • Cod Focaccia • Hot Mango and Kiwi with Ginger

2 hrs	45 mins	30 mins	15 mins
Prepare the cod for main course, cover and marinate, turning occasionally. Prepare the tomatoes and olives and reserve.	Prepare the appetizer for cooking. Prepare dessert for cooking, place in parcels and seal. Slice the focaccia for the main course.	Set beets to steam for 15 mins over dressing. Remove, peel and slice, place in serving dish. Transfer dressing to a small pan. • Remove fish from marinade, place in steamer with tomatoes and olives.	Set steamer to boil. Cook fish for 10–15 mins. Keep warm. Fry focaccia in butter and oil and keep warm. Heat dressing for beets, pour over and serve. Serve the fish and focaccia. Set the dessert to steam while eating main course.

MENU 5

• Mediterranean Artichokes • Pasta Primavera • Apricot Custard with Caramel Sauce

3 hrs	45 mins–1 hr	35–40 mins	30 mins
Prepare, steam and chill the dessert until ready to serve.	Prepare the ingredients for the appetizer, place in a foil parcel. Reserve.	Prepare the vegetables for the pasta and place in a steamer tier. Set salted water to boil in steamer base for the pasta.	Set artichokes to steam for 20 mins. Remove and serve onto warm plates. Put pasta in the steamer base and cook vegetables over the top for 10 mins while serving appetizer. Drain pasta and keep warm. Top with vegetables and serve. • Unmold the dessert, decorate and serve.

MENU 6

• Scallops in Creamy Saffron Sauce • Lamb with Port and Garlic • Charlotte Russe

4 hrs	1½ hrs	20 mins	10 mins
Soak the pears for the dessert for 20 mins. Prepare custard and line the mold. Assemble dessert, cover and steam for 40–50 mins. Chill completely in the refrigerator.	Prepare the scallops, marinate for 1 hr, turning occasionally. Place lamb in marinade. Cover and marinate for 1 hr, turning occasionally.	Place lamb sauce ingredients in a small pan. Set the steamer to boil. Remove the scallops from the marinade and place in steamer tier. Place sauce ingredients in a small pan. Make brandy cream for the dessert if serving.	Set the scallops to steam and the sauce to heat, serve as the appetizer. While serving scallops, set the lamb to cook, for 15–20 mins. Heat the sauce to serve. • Serve lamb garnished with rosemary. • Invert dessert and serve with brandy cream.

INDEX